MW01030150

The Disciples' Prayer

by
John MacArthur, Jr.

MOODY PRESS

CHICAGO

All Scripture quotations, unless noted otherwise, are from the *New Scofield Reference Bible*, King James Version. Copyright © 1967 by Oxford University Press, Inc. Reprinted by permission.

Library of Congress Cataloging in Publication Data

MacArthur, John.
  The disciples' prayer.

  (John MacArthur's Bible studies)
  Includes index.
  1. Lord's prayer. 2. Bible. N.T. Matthew VI,
9-15—Criticism, interpretation, etc. I. Title.
II. Series: MacArthur, John. Bible studies.
BV230.M228   1986   226'.9606   86-12721
ISBN 0-8024-5129-2 (pbk.)

2 3 4 5 6 7 Printing/EP/Year 91 90 89 88 87

Printed in the United States of America

Contents

These Bible studies are taken from messages delivered by Pastor-Teacher John MacArthur, Jr., at Grace Community Church in Panorama City, California. The recorded messages themselves may be purchased as a series or individually. Please request the current price list by writing to:

WORD OF GRACE COMMUNICATIONS
P.O. Box 4000
Panorama City, CA 91412

Or call the following toll-free number:
1-800-55-GRACE

1
The Purpose of Prayer

Outline

Introduction
A. The Importance of True Prayer
B. The Inadequacy of Unbiblical Prayer
C. The Instruction on True Prayer

Lesson
 I. The Jewish Perspective on Prayer
   A. The Historical Principles
     1. Prayer was a right
     2. Prayer was a weapon
     3. Prayer was heard
     4. Prayer was to be constant
     5. Prayer had certain elements
   B. The Hypocritical Practice
II. The Lord's Pattern of Prayer
   A. The Relationship Behind Prayer
   B. The Attitude of Prayer
   C. The Elements of Prayer

Conclusion

Introduction

For many people, the Disciples' Prayer—commonly known as the Lord's Prayer—is simply a prayer to recite. However, it is more than that. As we look at an overview of this prayer, you will see why. Doing a study on the Disciples' Prayer is a life-changing experience; it will impact a person's prayer life in the same way that the Beatitudes affect a person's commitment and consecration. There is much we can learn from the Disciples' Prayer. The prayer appears in Matthew 6:9-13: "Our Father, who art in heaven, hallowed be thy name. Thy kingdom come. Thy will be done in earth, as it is in heaven. Give us this day our daily bread. And forgive us our debts, as we forgive our debtors. And lead us not into temptation, but deliver us from evil. For thine is the kingdom, and the power, and the glory, forever. Amen."

In this portion of Scripture, we study one of the most important topics in the Christian life: prayer. The subject of prayer may seem overworked, but it is nonetheless vital. It is also a misunderstood subject. The believer must learn how to pray in order to experience the fullness of communion with God. The prayer Christ presents in Matthew 6:9-13 shows us how to pray. The importance of prayer is summed up in these words: "Pray without ceasing" (1 Thess. 5:17). Anything so consuming in the Christian life must be understood. If we don't know how to pray or what to pray for, then we don't profit from prayer. But if we do understand how to pray, then the command to pray without ceasing takes on greater significance.

In his gospel, Matthew presents Christ as King. In the Sermon on the Mount (Matt. 5-7), the King gave the standards of His kingdom. He contrasted His standards with those of the Jewish religious leaders. They thought their religious system was adequate to get them into the kingdom, but it wasn't. In Matthew 5, Jesus says their theology is not adequate, and in chapter 6 He says their religious activities and their view of the material world is not adequate. He illustrated the inadequacy of their religious activities by talking about their giving, praying, and fasting. He used those illustrations as a backdrop to reaffirm God's true standards regarding those activities. So what we see in Matthew 6 is a presentation of how a citizen of the kingdom is to live—not the way the Jewish people of that time lived.

A. The Importance of True Prayer

Of the three topics discussed in Matthew 6—giving, praying, and fasting—the greatest emphasis is placed on praying. Giving is important, but a person will give properly only when he has constant communion with God. Giving needs to be done with a heart filled with gratitude, which comes from a living communion with God. Fasting is also meaningless apart from prayer. Prayer must be a part of giving and fasting; that's why it is emphasized the most. Prayer is so essential that Martyn Lloyd-Jones said, "Man is at his greatest and highest when upon his knees he comes face to face with God" (*Studies in the Sermon on the Mount*, 2 vols. [Grand Rapids: Eerdmans, 1977], 2:45).

B. The Inadequacy of Unbiblical Prayer

In His discussion about prayer, Jesus challenged the manner in which people pray. He was saying, "Your prayers, just as your giving and fasting, are substandard." You may ask, "But wasn't Jesus talking only to the people of His time? How does this apply to us?" In many cases, religion is just as substandard and inadequate today as it was in Jesus' day. There are many people today who give to bring attention to themselves, fast so they will look holy, or pray pretentiously without recognizing the biblical standards for true prayer.

In Romans 8 the apostle Paul says Christians don't know what to pray for or how to pray. Then he says, "But the Spirit himself maketh intercession for us" (v. 26). We need God's help when we pray. Many Christians pray just as inadequately as non-Christians; many pray no differently than the Pharisees and scribes. So in His instruction on giving, fasting, and praying, the Lord spent most of His time on prayer. He didn't give many details on how we should give or fast, but He did give us a comprehensive description of how we are to pray. The Disciples' Prayer is a masterpiece from the infinite mind of an all-wise God, who encompassed every element of prayer in a simple pattern for prayer—all in sixty-six words. There are many different ways to view the Disciples' Prayer; we will examine them in our study.

Two Tests of True Spirituality

There are two ultimate tests of true spirituality: one is the study of God's Word, and the other is prayer. I believe the Bible confirms that studying God's Word should be first, because we don't know how to pray until we know what the Bible teaches about God, His will, our lives, and our problems. Knowledge gleaned from studying the Bible is what gives birth to a meaningful prayer life. You can't pray in a vacuum. A person who never has time to study the Bible because he prays all the time needs to cut the superfluousness from his prayers. It doesn't matter how long or short your prayer is; it's whether your prayer includes the necessary elements. You can say a short prayer or you can pray all night—the important thing is that your prayer include the necessary elements.

We must know God's Word before we can pray effectively. For example, there are people who plead with God to give them the Holy Spirit when they already have Him (Rom. 8:9; 1 Cor. 12:13). Some people pray for strength, yet the Bible says you can do all things through Christ, who strengthens you (Phil. 4:13). Some people pray, "Lord, be with us," but the Bible says, "Lo, I am with you always" (Matt. 28:20). There are people who ask God to help them love someone, when Romans 5:5 says, "The love of God is shed abroad in our hearts." People pray for things they already have, when they should be utilizing what God has

3

already given them. Unless we know the truths in Scripture, we won't know how to pray. Prayer is guided by a comprehension of God's truth. When we study His Word, we discover the real condition of our spiritual lives, and that drives us to open our hearts to God.

C. The Instruction on True Prayer

The Lord knew the importance of prayer. The Bible says that He would get up before dawn to pray (Mark 1:35). He also climbed the Mount of Olives to commune with the Father, sometimes praying all night long. The disciples saw in Jesus a tremendous commitment to prayer. That's probably what prompted them to say, "Lord, teach us to pray" (Luke 11:1). When they asked that question, He gave them the same pattern that appears in Matthew 6, even though it was a different occasion.

While Jesus was teaching in Matthew 6, He may have been telling the disciples, "Don't pray like the Pharisees do, trying to look pious before men. Don't pray in vain repetitions as pagans do. And don't pray with the idea that you're inform- ing God about what's happening in your life." Jesus knew if He said those things, the disciples would ask Him how they should pray. Presupposing that question, He begins in Matthew 6:9 with the pattern for true prayer. His teaching came at a marvelous time in the midst of the King's mani- festo. In the heart of the Sermon on the Mount, He set for all time the understanding that prayer is vital to a citizen of God's kingdom.

The Jewish religious leaders must have been stunned when Christ said their prayers were substandard. They gave prayer a high priority in their lives, but they didn't recognize that they had forsaken true prayer for routine religious exercises. They quoted set prayers in a ritualistic manner at different times of day. The Jews once knew the reality of genuine prayer but to a large extent lost it. Many people think the pattern for prayer in Matthew 6 is something new, but it isn't. Christ was reaffirming what the Old Testament stated. He began His sermon with these words: "Think not that I am come to destroy the law, or the prophets; I am not come to destroy, but to fulfill . . . one jot or one tittle shall in no way pass from the law, till all be fulfilled" (Matt. 5:17-18).

When Christ speaks about prayer in Matthew 6, He is affirming to the Jewish leaders things they should have already known.

4

Lesson

I. THE JEWISH PERSPECTIVE ON PRAYER

A. The Historical Principles

1. Prayer was a right

The Jews prayed to God because they believed God wanted them to come to Him. They didn't fear God the way pagans did. In fact, the rabbis said, "The Holy One yearns for the prayers of the righteous." Psalm 145:18 says, "The Lord is near unto all those who call upon him." In Psalm 91:15 the Lord says, "He shall call upon me, and I will answer him." The Jews learned from the Old Testament that God wanted to hear their prayers. Thus, they had no problem with the priority of prayer.

2. Prayer was a weapon

The rabbis believed that prayer wasn't just communication with God but that it released His power.

3. Prayer was heard

Psalm 65:2 reads, "O thou who hearest prayer, unto thee shall all flesh come." The Jews believed that God wanted to hear their prayers. However, those who worshiped Baal thought their god didn't care about their prayers. In 1 Kings 18:20-29, Elijah challenges those who worshiped Baal to call upon their god. They screamed to Baal, but nothing happened. Elijah told them to try harder, but still nothing happened. Even when they ripped off their clothes and cut their bodies, there was no response. They believed constant repetition of prayers was necessary to badger their gods into answering them. But the Jews who worshiped God believed He had a genuine interest in them.

The Midrash, the Jewish commentary on portions of the Old Testament, says this about Psalm 65:2: "A mortal man cannot grasp the conversation of two people speaking at the same time, but with God it is not so. All pray before Him, and He understands and receives all their prayers" (*Rabbah* 21.4). Men's ears become satisfied with hearing, but God's ears are never satiated. He is never wearied by men's prayers. God wants people to pray to Him. No matter how many other people are praying at the same time, He can hear your prayer, and He never gets tired of hearing from you.

4. Prayer was to be constant

The Jewish religious leaders taught people to avoid the habit of praying only when they were desperate. There are people who liken prayer to a parachute: They're glad it's there, and they hope they never have to use it. The Jewish leaders wanted people to pray all the time. The Talmud, the codification of rabbinic traditions, says, "Honour the physician *before* you have need of him. . . . The Holy One says, Just as it is my office to cause the rain and the dew to fall, and make the plants to grow to sustain man, so art thou bounden to pray before me, and to praise me in accordance with my works; thou shalt not say, I am in prosperity, wherefore shall I pray? But when misfortune befalls me then will I come and supplicate" (*Sanhedrin* 44*b*). So the Talmud is saying, before misfortune comes, anticipate and pray. Prayer is not to be used just for emergency appeals. It's to be an unbroken conversation built around a living, loving fellowship with God. The rabbis were right when they said that prayer was to be constant and that God could hear a multitude of prayers.

5. Prayer had certain elements

   a) Showing love and praise for God

   The Jewish people believed that prayer must include loving adoration and praise for God. The psalmist wrote, "I will bless the Lord at all times; his praise shall continually be in my mouth" (Ps. 34:1). Psalm 51:15 reads, "O Lord, open thou my lips, and my mouth shall show forth thy praise." Love and praise was to be incorporated in every prayer.

   b) Thanksgiving

   Jonah told the Lord, "I will sacrifice unto thee with the voice of thanksgiving" (2:9). The Jewish leaders taught that an important part of prayer was deep gratitude. The rabbis summed up the verses about thanksgiving in the Old Testament with this thought: "Though all prayers will one day be discontinued, the prayers of thanksgiving will never be discontinued." Someday we will no longer need to ask God for anything, and we will thank Him for everything.

c) Reverence

The Jewish people believed that their prayers should incorporate a sense of holiness and awe. They didn't flippantly rush into God's presence; they didn't treat God as if He were a man. They came before Him with reverence, recognizing that when they prayed, they were coming face-to-face with God. The prophet Isaiah saw the Lord in a vision "sitting upon a throne, high and lifted up, and his train filled the temple" (6:1). His response was, "I am a man of unclean lips, and I dwell in the midst of a people of unclean lips; for mine eyes have seen the King, the Lord of hosts" (v. 5). King David affirmed the majesty and holiness of God in his prayers before he made any requests. Rabbi Simon used to teach that in prayer, a man must see himself face-to face with the Shekinah.

d) Patient obedience

The Jewish people felt that a person should have a patient desire to obey God and that a person shouldn't pray unless his heart was right. It is wrong to approach God in a ritualistic, shallow manner, void of the desire to respond obediently to communion with God. Psalm 119 states that fact again and again. It's not right to rush into God's presence and say, "If things work out the way I want them to, I'll follow you." There were no conditions in the heart of a true Jew. He went to God with a spirit of obedience, saying, "God, whatever Your will is in this situation, I'll respond accordingly."

e) Confession

Godly Old Testament Jews knew that they were unclean and that when they came before God in prayer, they had to purge themselves of sin. They sensed their uncleanliness before God as Isaiah did (Isa. 6:5). King David knew he had to purge himself of his sins when he came into God's presence. In Psalm 26:6 he says, "I will wash mine hands in innocence; so will I compass thine altar, O Lord." Psalm 24 says, "Who shall ascend into the hill of the Lord? Or who shall stand in his holy place? He who hath clean hands, and a pure heart" (vv. 3-4). Only those who have dealt with their sin have the right to enter God's presence.

The rabbis said that when you weep over your sin, God hears your prayer. They also said that if you can bring nothing else to God, bring Him your tears, and He will hear you. The Jews believed that God responded to the prayers of righteous people. James 5:16 says, "The effectual, fervent prayer of a righteous man availeth much." The Jews said the prayer of a pure heart overturned the wrath of God as a rake overturns grain. They believed you could turn wrath into mercy when you had a pure heart.

f) Unselfishness

The Jews had a sense of community that we don't really understand. They saw themselves as a nation; they were a theocracy ruled by God. The fact that Israel still exists as a nation today shows how vitally the Jewish people have clung to the preservation of their national identity. When they prayed, they took their community into consideration. They didn't pray in a self-centered manner. The rabbis asked God not to listen to the prayer of a traveler. That's because when a person went on a journey, he would say, "Lord, while I'm on my journey, please bring good weather. Don't let there be rain or snow; let me have an easy journey." But the rabbis didn't want the Lord to answer such a prayer because an ignorant traveler may ask for a fair day in a region where people needed rain for their crops. The rabbis wanted God to do what needed to be done for the good of everyone, not just a selfish traveler.

Many of us come to God with personal pronouns in our prayers: me, myself, and I. We share with the Lord our needs and problems without thinking of others in the Body of Christ. God has a master plan for His kingdom, and sometimes we have to sacrifice what might seem best for ourselves because God has a greater plan for the whole. We don't always have the right perspective on prayer. A true believing Jew in the Old Testament prayed for whatever advanced God's cause among His people, not for his own personal gain. Many of us have developed a self-centeredness in prayer that is unbiblical. We isolate ourselves, don't communicate with others, and don't bear one another's burdens. Consequently, our prayers have a narrow focus. We need to pray unselfishly for whatever is best for the whole. That's why there are no singular personal pronouns in the Disciples' Prayer in Matthew 6. The word *our* is used because true prayer encompasses the community of faith.

g) Perseverance

True believing Old Testament Jews taught that prayer was to be persistent. In 2 Corinthians 12:7, the apostle Paul prays for the Lord to remove "a thorn in the flesh." When the first request was denied, He persevered and prayed two more times. Deuteronomy 9 tells us that after the Israelites had worshiped the golden calf, Moses prayed for forty days over the people's sin (vv. 25-26). He persevered in prayer.

h) Humility

A true Jew went before the Lord in prayer to submit to the will of God. The greatest illustration of that comes from the truest Jew who ever lived: Jesus. In His prayer in the Garden of Gethsemane, He said to the Father, "Not my will, but thine, be done" (Luke 22:42). When we pray, instead of asking the Lord to do our will, we should conform ourselves to His will. We are to ask God to do His will and to give us the grace to enjoy it.

All the above elements were part of the prayer life of true believing Jews in the Old Testament. They had an intense commitment to prayer. One rabbi said that a man could not come into the presence of God unless he brought his heart in his hands. They had a great heritage of prayer.

B. The Hypocritical Practice

During the Old Testament age up to the time of Christ, many Jewish people developed a wrong perspective on prayer. Their prayers became hypocritical. In Matthew 6:5, Christ says the Jewish religious leaders loved to pray "standing in the synagogues and at the corners of the streets, that they may be seen by men." Their prayers were phony; they weren't talking to God, they were selfishly making a public display, saying vain repetitions in the hope that God would do things their way if they prayed long enough. Verse 8 implies that the religious leaders prayed as if they had to keep God informed about what was going on.

II. THE LORD'S PATTERN OF PRAYER

In Matthew 6:9-13, Jesus reaffirms the definition of prayer. He included the ingredients of prayer from Old Testament Jewish tradition. He didn't say anything new, although He gave new richness to everything He said. Since many of us don't know how to pray any better than the Jewish leaders did, we need to study what the Lord had to say about prayer.

Is the Disciples' Prayer to Be Recited?

Many people misunderstand the Lord's instruction regarding prayer in Matthew 6. Instead of learning how to pray from the Disciples' Prayer, we recite it. However, it's not a prayer to be recited but a pattern for all prayer. Let me explain why.

The Disciples' Prayer is recorded twice in Scripture: in Matthew 6 and in Luke 11. In both accounts, the prayer is substantially the same, but the words are different. If the Lord was giving us a prayer to be memorized, He wouldn't have used different words in the two passages. For example, in Matthew 6:12 He says, "Forgive us our debts," but in Luke 11:4 He says, "forgive us our sins."

In Luke 11:1 the disciples say to Jesus, "Teach us to pray." They didn't say, "Teach us a prayer." There is a difference between reading from a prayer book and knowing how to pray.

In Matthew 6:7 the Lord says, "When ye pray, use not vain repetitions, as the pagans do." Would He have given us a prayer to recite right after saying that? No. He was saying we should avoid vain repetition.

There is no other place in the entire New Testament where the Disciples' Prayer is recited. It is a model to pattern your prayers after; it is a skeleton that you are to put meat on. For example, when I preach, I have my sermon notes in front of me. If I just read my notes to you, my message would be only ten minutes long. I have to add content to my notes to make my message come alive. Christ was giving us an outline to pray by in Matthew 6. We have to add meaningful expression to our prayers each time we pray.

The Disciples' Prayer is a model for all prayers. If you memorize the pattern this prayer presents to us and use it each time you pray, you'll have confidence that you're praying the way Jesus taught us to pray. There are different facets to this prayer; let's look at them.

A. The Relationship Behind Prayer

The Disciples' Prayer reveals the different aspects of our relationship with God.

   1. "Our Father"—Father/child relationship

   2. "Hallowed be thy name"—Deity/worshiper relationship

   3. "Thy kingdom come"—Sovereign/subject relationship

   4. "Thy will be done"—Master/servant relationship

   5. "Give us . . . our daily bread"—Benefactor/beneficiary relationship

   6. "Forgive us our debts"—Savior/sinner relationship

   7. "Lead us not into temptation"—Guide/pilgrim relationship

B. The Attitude of Prayer

The Disciples' Prayer indicates what our attitude should be when we pray.

   1. "Our"—An unselfish spirit

   2. "Father"—A familial spirit

   3. "Hallowed be thy name"—A reverent spirit

   4. "Thy kingdom come"—A loyal spirit

   5. "Thy will be done"—A submissive spirit

   6. "Give us . . . our daily bread"—A dependent spirit

   7. "Forgive us our debts"—A penitent spirit

   8. "Lead us not into temptation"—A humble spirit (& teachable spirit)

   9. "Thine is the kingdom"—A confident spirit

   10. "And the power"—A triumphant spirit

   11. "And the glory"—An exultant spirit

C. The Elements of Prayer

   1. The priority in prayer

      This prayer can be divided into two sets of three elements each. The first three elements ("Hallowed be thy name," "Thy kingdom come," "Thy will be done") deal with God's glory, and the second three ("Give us our daily bread," "Forgive us our debts," "Lead us not into temptation") deal with man's need. When you set God in His rightful place in your prayers, everything else will flow from there. All prayer is to begin with the character of God. When God is first, prayer makes sense.

2. The purpose of prayer

The first three elements in the Disciples' Prayer discuss the purpose of prayer: (1) to honor the name of God, (2) to bring His kingdom to earth, and (3) to do His will. What are the means by which His name is hallowed, His kingdom lifted up, and His will done? As God provides our daily bread, pardons our sins, and protects us when we are tempted, He is exalted in His glory, kingdom, and will.

3. The recipient of prayer

The Disciples' Prayer begins with these words: "Our Father . . . hallowed be thy name." God is our Father. He is also a King, as indicated by the statement, "Thy kingdom come." The phrase "thy will be done" recognizes God as our Master. As a Father, He gives us our daily bread; as a King, He forgives our debts; and as a Master, He protects us in the midst of temptation.

4. The comprehensiveness of prayer

Let's look at the last three elements in the prayer. Giving us our daily bread (provision), granting us forgiveness (pardon), and not leading us into temptation (protection) deal with the three temporal dimensions of life: "our daily bread" has to do with the present; "forgive us our debts" refers to our past sins; and "lead us not into temptation" looks to future protection. The Disciples' Prayer encompasses the past, present, and future sustenance of God. Also, bread speaks of our physical needs, forgiveness relieves the mental anguish of guilt, and protection in the midst of temptation deals with our spiritual needs.

5. The intensity of prayer

All the petitions in this prayer are in the imperative mode in the Greek text, which means there's an intensity to them. Although each phrase is brief, the imperative mode conveys intensity.

Conclusion

The elements and wonders of the model of prayer Christ gave us are almost infinite. Only the mind of God could have conceived such far-reaching thoughts and compressed them into this small portion of Scripture. No man could have ever done that.

Prayer is not to be used in an attempt to bend the will of God to your desire. Prayer will bend you to fit the will of God. We should acknowledge God's sovereignty when we pray. This is what our perspective should be: "God, give me my daily bread only if it hallows Your name. Pardon my sins only if that exalts Your kingdom. Lead me not into temptation if that lets You be the Master in my life." The purpose of all prayer is to glorify God. The Disciples' Prayer ends by saying, "For thine is the kingdom, and the power, and the glory, forever" (v. 13). Everything in the Disciples' Prayer seeks to glorify God and lift up His name.

Prayer is not for our benefit. Many people get confused in their prayer lives because they think prayer is for themselves, and they don't take into account the community of believers and the will of God. In John 14:13 Jesus says, "Whatever ye shall ask in my name, that will I do, that the Father may be glorified in the Son." The reason we pray and God answers our prayers is so that God may put His glory on display. So when you pray, don't do it just to inform God about what is happening in your life. Don't pray in an attempt to badger Him to do what you want Him to do. The Disciples' Prayer affirms that we should enter God's presence in submission to His sovereignty. The prayer begins by adoring God ("Our Father, who art in heaven") and ends the same way ("For thine is the kingdom, and the power, and the glory, forever"). The entire prayer recognizes God's sovereignty. Prayer is to bring glory to God.

Focusing on the Facts

1. What does Christ talk about in Matthew 6? On what did He place the greatest emphasis (see p. 2)?
2. Explain what Paul says in Romans 8:26 concerning our prayers (see p. 3).
3. What are two things that indicate a person's spirituality? Why is the presence of one necessary for the other (see p. 3)?
4. Describe the Lord's commitment to prayer (see p. 4).
5. What had happened to the prayers of the Jewish people over time (see p. 4)?
6. Why did the Jews pray to God (see p. 5)?
7. Contrast the Jewish and pagan perspectives on whether deity actually heard and wanted to respond to prayer (see p. 5).
8. What does the Midrash have to say about God and prayer (see p. 5)?
9. According to the Jewish religious leaders, how frequently were people to pray? Explain (see p. 6).
10. How did Isaiah react when he was before the Lord? What did

King David do in his prayers before he made any requests (see p. 7)?

11. How is obedience expressed in prayer (see p. 7)?

12. Explain and illustrate the unselfish nature of the prayers of true believing Jewish people. How does that contrast with the way man people pray today (see pp. 8-9)?

13. What elements did believing Jews say should be present in prayer (see pp. 6-9)?

14. What should we do with our sin when we come before God? What does Scripture say about that (see pp. 7-8)?

15. How should we express humility in our prayers (see p. 9)?

16. How do we know that the Disciples' Prayer isn't to be recited (see p. 10)?

17. What aspects of our relationship with God does the Disciples' Prayer mention (see p. 11)?

18. What should be our attitude when we come before God in prayer (see p. 11)?

19. What is the purpose of prayer (see p. 12)?

20. Discuss the comprehensiveness of the Disciples' Prayer (see p. 12).

21. The reason we pray and God _____our prayers is so that God may put His _____on _____(see p. 13).

Pondering the Principles

1. When you study God's Word, do you allow yourself time to respond in prayer about what you've just learned? Think of some ways you would benefit by doing that. Since the Bible is God's message to us, when we pray about what we've read, we will be responding in a direct way to what God is teaching us. Develop a habit of making prayer a part of your study time.

2. The Jewish religious leaders of Christ's time used to pray standing "in the synagogues and in the streets, that they may have glory from men" (Matt. 6:2). Interestingly, many Christians today have the opposite problem: They're ashamed of praying before other people in a restaurant or in other public places. Why is that so? What positive results could come about from not being ashamed to pray in public?

3. How often do you pray, and what is usually the content of your prayers? Does the content of your prayers vary from day to day? It's easy to fall into the trap of letting prayer be a duty and not a

joy. Reread the section about the elements of prayer on pages 11-12. Are those elements present in your prayers? Work on making each of those elements a regular part of your prayers, and think about what some of the results would be.

2
The Paternity of Prayer

Outline

Introduction
A. The Priorities of a Believer
B. The Prayers of a Believer
1. The particulars of prayer
    (*a*) The posture of prayer
    (*b*) The place of prayer
    (*c*) The time of prayer
    (*d*) The circumstances of prayer
2. The preface to prayer
3. The perspective of prayer

Lesson
I. God's Paternity (v. 9*a*)
A. Explaining the Principle
1. Abolishing a misunderstanding
2. Affirming the truth
B. Examining the Perspectives
1. The Jewish viewpoint on prayer
    a) From the Old Testament era
        (1) The begetting of God
        (2) The nearness of God
        (3) The grace of God
        (4) The guidance of God
        (5) Obedience to God
    b) From the New Testament era
2. The Greek and Roman viewpoints on prayer
    a) The Stoics
    b) The Epicureans
3. The modern-day viewpoint on prayer
4. The biblical viewpoint on prayer
    a) The statement
    b) The significance
        (1) The end of fear

    (2) The provision of hope

    (3) The end of loneliness

    (4) The end of selfishness

    (5) The availability of resources

    (6) The requirement for obedience

    (7) The source of wisdom

Introduction

The Disciples' Prayer in Matthew 6:9-13 reads, "Our Father, who art in heaven, hallowed be thy name. Thy kingdom come. Thy will be done in earth, as it is in heaven. Give us this day our daily bread. And forgive us our debts, as we forgive our debtors. And lead us not into temptation, but deliver us from evil. For thine is the kingdom, and the power, and the glory, forever. Amen."

A. The Priorities of a Believer

There are two spiritual activities that should never cease in a believer's life—two great pillars that hold a Christian up in his daily living: the study of God's Word and prayer. In Acts 6:4 the apostles say, "We will give ourselves continually to prayer, and to the ministry of the word." When we pray, we speak to God; when we study the Bible, the Lord speaks to us.

The Bible and prayer make up the interchange between man and God. Scripture says we are to be unceasingly involved in both activities. In the Pentateuch we read that God's will was for man to talk of the law when he stood up, laid down, and walked around during the day (Deut. 6:6-7). We are to meditate on the law of God day and night (Ps. 1:2). The Word of God should continually be in our thoughts and conversations. The same is true about prayer. The apostle Paul said, "Pray without ceasing" (1 Thess. 5:17). In Ephesians 6:18 he writes that we are to pray "always with all prayer and supplication in the Spirit." Philippians 4:6 says, "In everything, by prayer and supplication with thanksgiving, let your requests be made known unto God."

We are to pray at all times, and we are to study the Word, meditate on it, and talk about it. Prayer and Bible study are to be the consuming elements of a believer's life. For example, George Mueller, a great man of prayer, was asked how much time he spent in prayer. His reply was, "I live in the spirit of prayer. I pray as I walk, when I lie down, and when I rise. The answers are always coming." For him, prayer was a way of   life.

B. The Prayers of a Believer

Our Lord knew that prayer was to be a way of life for the believer. In the Sermon on the Mount, when He compared the false religious standard of the scribes and Pharisees to the true standard of God, He interjected a word of instruction on the matter of proper prayer. Since prayer is such an important part of a Christian's life, we need to know how to pray. In Luke 11, Christ gives the same pattern of prayer as He does in Matthew 6 when the disciples say, "Lord, teach us to pray" (v. 1). In the Lord's teaching on prayer, notice what He *doesn't* discuss.

1. The particulars of prayer

    a) The posture of prayer

    Any posture will do for prayer. In the Bible, people prayed standing (Gen. 24:12-14), lifting up their hands (1 Tim. 2:8), sitting (Judg. 20:26), kneeling (Mark 1:40), looking upward (John 17:1), bowing down (Ex. 34:8), placing their heads between their knees (1 Kings 18:42), pounding on their breasts (Luke 18:13), and facing the Temple (Dan. 6:10).

    b) The place of prayer

    In the Bible, we read that people can pray anywhere: in battle (2 Chron. 13:14-15), in a cave (1 Kings 19:9-10), in a closet (Matt. 6:6), in a garden (Matt. 26:36-44), on a mountainside (Luke 6:12), by a river (Acts 16:13), by the sea (Acts 21:5-6), in the street (Matt. 6:5), in the Temple (1 Kings 8:22-53), in bed (Ps. 4:3-4), in a home (Acts 9:39-40), in the stomach of a fish (Jonah 2:1-10), on a housetop (Acts 10:9), in a prison (Acts 16:23-26), in the wilderness (Luke 5:16), and on a cross (Luke 23:33-34, 46). In 1 Timothy 2:8 Paul says, "I will . . . that men pray everywhere."

    c) The time of prayer

    I remember hearing a man tell a group of ministers that the Bible teaches we should pray in the morning. I examined the Bible and found that people prayed not just in the morning but also three times a day (Dan. 6:10), in the evening (1 Kings 18:36), before meals (Matt. 14:19), after meals (Deut. 8:10), at the ninth hour (3:00 P.M.; Acts 3:1), at bedtime (Ps. 4:4), at midnight (Acts 16:25), day and night (Luke 2:37; 18:7), often (Luke 5:33), when they're young

(Jer. 3:4), when they're old (Dan. 9:2-19), when they're in trouble (2 Kings 19:3-4), every day (Ps. 86:3), and always (Luke 18:1; 1 Thess. 5:17).

d) The circumstances of prayer

Some people think they should have on their prayer shawls when they pray. Orthodox Jewish people today have to dress properly before they pray. But the Bible documents people praying in many different circumstances. They prayed wearing sackcloth (Ps. 35:13), sitting in ashes (Job 1:20-21; 2:8), smiting their breasts (Luke 18:13), crying (Ps. 6:6), throwing dust on their heads (Josh. 7:6), tearing their garments (1 Kings 21:27), fasting (Deut. 9:18), sighing (Ezra 9:4-15), groaning (Ps. 6:4-6), crying out loud (Heb. 5:7), sweating blood (Luke 22:44), agonizing with broken hearts (Ps. 34:18), making a vow (Acts 18:18), making sacrifices (Ps. 20:1-3), and singing songs (Acts 16:25).

Prayer is fitting at any time, in any posture, in any place, under any circumstance, and in any attire. Prayer is to be a total way of life; it is an open communion with God that continues at all times. Sometimes it will be more intense than at other times, but it should be continual. If that's the case, then we need to understand how to pray, and that's precisely what Jesus teaches us in Matthew 6.

After This Manner, Pray Ye

The Lord preceded His model prayer with these words: "After this manner, therefore, pray ye" (Matt. 6:9). The first phrase is *houtōs oun* in the Greek text and literally means "thus or therefore." It could be translated "along these lines." So Jesus wasn't saying, "pray using these exact words." The Greek word *houtōs* also appears in Acts 13:34, which is a paraphrase of Isaiah 55:3. So, *houtōs* doesn't mean "in these exact words" but refers more to the general content of a statement. Many people have recited the Disciples' Prayer over and over in a meaningless way, yet the Lord intended it to be a skeletal outline for all prayer.

The major thrust of the prayer is that it focuses on the glory of God. All prayer should do that. We should pray to the Lord not in an attempt to get Him to do our will but to affirm His sovereignty and make our will submissive to His. In John 14:13 Jesus says, "Whatever ye shall ask in my name, that will I do, that the Father may be glorified. We are not to use prayer to get what we want but to put God's majesty on display. All prayer should focus on God.

2. The preface to prayer

In the Old Testament, true saints of God worshiped Him before they began their prayers, no matter how severe their circumstances. For example, Jonah prayed to the Lord from the belly of a great fish. I'm sure that was a fearful, miserable experience. In Jonah 2, when he begins to pray to the Lord, he could have dispensed with the amenities and simply said, "Get me out of here, God!" But Jonah began with a marvelous anthem of worship and praise. He knew no man could ask God for something unless he affirmed that the Lord has the sovereign right to say yes or no to a request. That's the basis for prayer; our will is to be brought into submission with God's will.

Daniel was always on the precipice of disaster because of the strategic place he held in the midst of the pagan Babylonian society. In Daniel 9:3-4, in his concern over Judah's captivity, he prays to the Lord and affirms His majesty, glory, dignity, holiness, and almighty character. In Jeremiah 32 the prophet Jeremiah, who spent much of his time in frustration weeping brokenheartedly over his people, pours out a prayer to the Lord and recites attribute after attribute of God's majesty (vv. 16-23).

3. The perspective of prayer

Why did the Old Testament saints worship God at the beginning of their prayers? Why does the Disciples' Prayer begin, "Our Father, who art in heaven, hallowed be thy name"; "Thy kingdom come"; "Thy will be done" and end, "for thine is the kingdom, and the power, and the glory, forever"? Because prayer is to give God the privilege of displaying His majesty. We are to pray to bring our lives into harmony with His will.

In Psalm 86 David prays to God, seeking His mercy, love, and compassion. However, he didn't begin his prayer with a petition. In verses 6-7 he says, "Give ear, O Lord, unto my prayer, and attend to the voice of my supplications. In the day of my trouble I will call upon thee; for thou wilt answer me." Although David was in the midst of trouble and was filled with anxiety, he prayed these words: "Among the gods there is none like unto thee, O

Lord; neither are there any works like unto thy works"
(v. 8). Notice that David began by affirming the majesty
and character of God. Verses 9-10 continue, "All nations
whom thou hast made shall come and worship before
thee, O Lord, and shall glorify thy name. For thou art
great, and doest wondrous things; thou art God alone."

The Old Testament saints knew that in their prayers, they
were to set God in His rightful place and bring their wills
into conformity with His. David does that in Psalm 86:11.
He says, "Teach me thy way, O Lord; I will walk in thy
truth." That is not a request. First, David acknowledged
God's sovereignty; then he indicated a willingness to
submit to His will. Verse 11 ends, "Unite my heart to fear
thy name." In other words, "Make my heart one with
Your heart." Prayer is bowing submissively to the will of
God. Then in verse 12 David says, "I will praise thee, O
Lord my God, with all my heart, and I will glorify thy
name for evermore." You can't separate prayer from
praise.

Lesson

Every statement in the Disciples' Prayer focuses on God. Let's look
briefly at the outline of this prayer as we begin our lesson: "Our
Father, who art in heaven" speaks of God's paternity. "Hallowed be
thy name" speaks of God's priority. "Thy kingdom come" refers to
God's program. "Thy will be done" talks about God's purpose. "Give
us this day our daily bread" refers to God's provision. "Forgive us our
debts, as we forgive our debtors" speaks of God's pardon. "Lead us
not into temptation, but deliver us from evil" talks about God's
protection. And "thine is the kingdom, and the power, and the glory,
forever" refers to God's preeminence.

I. GOD'S PATERNITY (v. 9a)

"Our Father, who art in heaven."

If you think about it, the term *Father* is probably one of the most
commonly used terms in our prayers. It should be, for that's the
pattern Jesus sets. Prayer begins with a recognition that God is
our Father.

A. Explaining the Principle

1. Abolishing a misunderstanding

The word *our* in Matthew 6:9 refers to believers. That is a
blow to the liberal teaching concerning the fatherhood of

22

God and brotherhood of man. for years, liberal theologians have taught that God is everyone's Father, and that we are all brothers. However, God is everyone's Father only in the sense of creation. Malachi 2:10 says, "Have we not all one father? Hath not one God created us?" We are one in the sense that God created us. In Acts 17:28 Paul says this to philosophers on Mars' Hill: "We are . . . his offspring."

Although God is our Father through creation, that doesn't mean everyone has a relationship with Him as Father. In John 8:44 Jesus tells the Jewish religious leaders, "Ye are of your father the devil." In 1 John 3:7-10, the apostle John makes a distinction between children of God and children of the devil. The former do not continue to commit sin, but the latter do. Paul talks about "children of light" in Ephesians 5:8. Mankind is not one big family under the universal fatherhood of God. Rather, there are two families in the world: the children of God and the children of the devil. Second Peter 1:4 says that only believers are "partakers of the divine nature." John 1:12 says, "As many as received him [Christ], to them gave he power to become the children of God." When Jesus uses the word "our" in the phrase "our Father" in Matthew 6:9, He eliminates all the unbelieving people.

2. Affirming the truth

The phrase "our Father" affirms a wonderful intimacy with God that is known only by believers. Most of the people in the world who worship other gods view those gods as distant beings to be feared. Even the Jewish people of Christ's time thought God was remote. The Old Testament Jewish believers understood the fatherhood of God more in terms of God's overall care of the nation Israel than they did in an intimate, personal sense. It wasn't until Jesus came to earth that men really saw God as a personal Father. That is clearly illustrated for us in John 14:8, where Philip says to Jesus, "Show us the Father." Jesus responded, "Have I been such a long time with you, and yet hast thou not known me, Philip? He that hath seen me hath seen the Father" (v. 9). Christ brought to us awareness of the intimate relationship we can have with God.

B. Examining the Perspectives

    1. The Jewish viewpoint on prayer

        a) From the Old Testament era

The Old Testament Jews understood God's fatherhood in the sense of His care for their nation. By the time Jesus came into the world, they had largely lost the concept of God as Father. As they moved away from true religion and worship by establishing a system that tolerated their sinfulness, they cut themselves off from God's fatherly care. Consequently the Jews assumed God was remote, and it became blasphemous even to mention the name of God. So when the Lord used the term "our Father" at the beginning of His model on prayer, the Jewish religious leaders were shocked. They were awakened to a new intimacy with God that they had never understood.

The Jews in the Old Testament era did understand the fatherhood of God. In Isaiah 64 the prophet makes a statement regarding the sinfulness of the Israelites. He says, "We have sinned . . . we are all as an unclean thing, and all our righteousnesses are as filthy rags; and we all do fade as a leaf, and our iniquities, like the wind, have taken us away. And there is none that calleth upon thy name, that stirreth up himself to take hold of thee; for thou hast hidden thy face from us, and hast consumed us, because of our iniquities" (vv. 5-7). The nation of Israel felt lost. They were evil and didn't seek God. Then in verse 8 Isaiah says, "But now, O Lord, thou art our father." He reaffirmed the comforting reality that God is their Father. And fathers take care of their children.

The Jews of the Old Testament saw five basic elements in the fatherhood of God:

    (1) The begetting of God

God was a Father in terms of His begetting. First Chronicles 29:10 gives Him the title, "Lord God of Israel, our father." He was the One who had fathered the nation.

    (2) The nearness of God

In family relationships, a father is closer than an uncle or a cousin. He's also closer than a friend or a neighbor. The Old Testament Jews saw nearness in the term *Father*. That is illustrated in Psalm 68, which talks about God's power. There, we read of God being on a high hill (vv. 15-16) and in the heavens (v. 33) and that He has twenty thousand chariots and many angels (v. 17). Yet in the midst of that narrative, we read that God is "a father of the fatherless" (v. 5). The Jews knew the majesty of God and thought of Him as somewhat remote, but they also knew He was a Father to the fatherless.

(3) The grace of God

A father is forgiving, tenderhearted, merciful, and gracious to his children. God is such a Father, as we learn from Psalm 103:13: "As a father pitieth his children, so the Lord pitieth them that fear him." God is a condescending, gracious, gentle Father, and that's how the Old Testament Jews saw Him.

(4) The guidance of God

A father leads his children and gives them wisdom and instruction. In Jeremiah 31:9 God says, "They [the people of Israel] shall come with weeping, and with supplications will I lead them; I will cause them to walk by the rivers of waters in a straight way, in which they shall not stumble; for I am a father to Israel." He was saying that He would guide the Israelites and make sure they didn't fall. Why? Because He was their Father, and a father guides his children.

(5) Obedience to God

None of the other four elements of the fatherhood of God sentimentalized the Old Testament Jews to the Lord because of their viewpoint on obeying Him. They saw God as One who begot them and would stay near, be gracious, and be a guide to them when they were obedient to Him. When the Israelites had been sinful, they were told, "Do ye thus requite the Lord, O foolish people and unwise? Is not he thy father who hath bought thee?" (Deut. 32:6). You can't treat a father with disobedience and disrespect.

b) From the New Testament era

The Old Testament Jews saw God as a Father in a general sense. He begat, loved, and guided them, and they knew they were responsible to obey Him. In the Sermon on the Mount, Jesus confirms that when He says, "Ask, and it shall be given you; seek, and ye shall find; knock, and it shall be opened unto you; for every one that asketh receiveth; and he that seeketh findeth; and to him that knocketh it shall be opened. Or what man is there of you whom, if his son ask bread, will he give him a stone? Or if he ask a fish, will he give him a serpent? If ye then, being evil, know how to give good gifts unto your children, how much more shall your Father, who is in heaven, give good things to them that ask him?" (Matt. 7:7-11). Christ reintroduced His Jewish audience to the fact that God is a beneficent, loving Father. He takes care of the needs of His children.

To many Jews of the New Testament era, the term *Father* as applied to God had lost its meaning. For the Pharisees and scribes to think of God as Father meant no more than to think of Him as a lord, ruler, or king. In the Sermon on the Mount, Jesus injects a rich, intimate meaning into the concept of God as Father, especially because He brought God to men. He made such intimacy possible.

A Unique Father/Child Relationship

When Jesus prayed, He always used the term *Father*. Only once did He ever pray and not use that term, and that was when He said, "My God, my God, why hast thou forsaken me?" (Matt. 27:46). When Christ bore the sins of the world, He was separated from the Father. But in all His other prayers, Christ expressed the intimacy of His relationship to the Father. When we pray "our Father" we are not addressing some beneficent character. Nor are we talking to a deity who is totally unconcerned about us—a father in terms of leadership only. God is our Father in a loving, personal way.

2. The Greek and Roman viewpoints on prayer

There are two major groups of philosophers in the Greek and Roman world of Christ's time: the Stoics and the Epicureans.

a) The Stoics

The Stoics taught that one attribute of all the gods was apathy. The Greeks defined apathy (Gk., *apatheia*) as an inability to experience any feelings. They taught that if a person could feel love, he could be hurt; and that if he could feel joy, he could feel sadness. Thus they concluded that the gods could not be influenced by people to feel hurt or unhappy, therefore they were totally indifferent and devoid of passion or feelings.

b) The Epicureans

The Epicureans said the supreme quality of the deities was *ataraxia*, which means "complete calm" or "perfect peace." They said that if the gods got involved in human affairs, they would not be able to maintain their serenity. Therefore, they were detached. This deistic view says that there is a power who created everything, put everything into motion, and then walked away because it didn't want to get involved. The Epicureans saw the gods as totally isolated from every human condition.

3. The modern-day viewpoint on prayer

Poet Thomas Hardy said that prayer is useless because there's no one to pray to except "that dreaming, dark, dumb thing that turns the handle of this idle show." Voltaire said life was "a bad joke." He continued, "Bring down the curtain; the farce is done." H. G. Wells, in one of his novels, painted a picture of a man defeated by the stress of modern life. The man was dying, and he was told by his doctor that his only hope was to find fellowship with God. The man responded, "What? That—up there—having fellowship with me? I would as soon think of cooling my throat with the Milky Way or shaking hands with the stars."

The Stoic saw the gods as being emotionless, and the Epicureans saw them as being detached. Some people today see God as the dreaming, dumb thing that turns the handle of the idle show, and even the Jews of Christ's time saw God as a Father only in a remote sense. In all that confusion, Jesus simply uttered without explanation these two words: "Our Father." In doing so, He opened marvelous new dimensions of the meaning of *Father*.

4. The biblical viewpoint on prayer

    a) The statement

    The Greek word for "father" is *pater*, but there's little doubt in my mind that Christ used the Aramaic term *Abba*, an endearing term used by a little child speaking to his father. The Talmud says that one of the first words a Jewish child learned to say was *Abba*. Jesus uses that term in Mark 14:36 when he says, "Abba, Father. . . . Take away this cup from me." According to Romans 8:15 and Galatians 4:6, we can cry out to the Lord, "Abba, Father." That's different from the Jewish perspective of God as a deity responsible for the whole nation. God isn't indifferent toward us; we can come to Him in an intimate relationship. Arabs today still use the term *abba* to refer to daddy or papa. The viewpoint of God as an intimate Father differs from the viewpoints of the Pharisees, philosophers, and skeptics.

    b) The significance

    What is significant about the fact that God is our Father?

    (1) The end of fear

    Missionaries say that one of the greatest gifts that Christianity brings to primitive societies is the certainty that God is a loving, caring Father. Many people living in such societies fear their gods. Many of those living under the influence of false religions lived in absolute fear until they came to know the loving Father by putting their faith in Christ. The gods of many societies are characterized by jealousy, hostility, and vengeance. That's why the phrase "our Father" in Matthew 6:9 is so wonderful; it puts an end to fear.

    (2) The provision of hope

    The world is hostile. When you break the unchangeable laws God has established, you sin—and the wages of sin is death (Rom. 6:23). No wonder Voltaire said life was a bad joke. He had no hope because he didn't know the loving Father.

When I was a child, my dad dropped me off at a street corner and said, "Wait for me; I will come back and get you." I waited for a while, and he didn't come to pick me up. Even when it started getting dark outside, I saw no sight of him. During that time, he had car trouble, and that's what kept him from returning. By the time he was able to pick me up, the stores had long been closed, and it was very dark. He hugged me and asked if I was upset at him, and I said, "No. You told me you'd come back, and I was just waiting for you." That's the hope a child has in his father, and that's the hope we Christians have in the midst of a hostile world that is falling apart. God is our Father, and He will take care of us.

(3) The end of loneliness

Lonely people need to know that God is a Father. Many people experience loneliness, bitterness, self-despair, and self-pity in their lives. They need respect. Where can we get that? Is there anyone who can lift us up and make us feel like we have a friend? God can; He's our Father. He said, "Lo, I am with you always" (Matt. 28:20). The fatherhood of God settles the matter of loneliness.

(4) The end of selfishness

In Matthew 6:9 Jesus says, "Our Father," not "My Father." Prayer isn't selfish; it always embraces the community of faith. There are not singular personal pronouns in the Disciples' Prayer. When you pray, do so with your arms around everyone else, not just yourself. Ephesians 6:18 says we are to pray always "with all prayer and supplication . . . for all saints." Don't just pray for yourself. God is not just your Father or my Father; He's *our* Father. The use of the word *our* in Matthew 6:9 ends all claims to exclusiveness.

(5) The availability of resources

The Disciples' Prayer begins, "Our Father, who art in heaven." God draws our resources not from the world but from heaven. He has the supernatural domain at His disposal. All that heaven is and all that it means to be blessed "with all spiritual blessings in heavenly places" (Eph. 1:3) is available through knowing God. Commentator Arthur Pink said, "If God is in heaven then prayer needs to be a thing of the heart and not of the lips, for no physical voice on earth can rend the skies, but sighs and groans will reach the ears of God. If we are to pray to God in heaven, then our souls must be detached from all of earth. If we pray to God in heaven, then faith must wing our petitions" (*An Exposition on the Sermon on the Mount* [Grand Rapids: Baker, 1974], p. 161). Heaven is not so much a place as it is a dimension of God's supernatural resources. Do you want satisfaction? God has it at His disposal. If you want fairness, peace, fellowship, knowledge, victory, and boldness, He can give them to you. We pray to a Father who has eternal resources.

(6) The requirement for obedience

Children used to have respect for their fathers. That's disappearing now. In the Old Testament, God said to stone disobedient children (Deut. 21:18-21). He wants the world to know that children are to obey their parents. Likewise, we are to obey God our Father. If the Bible teaches that children are to obey their earthly parents, how much more should we obey God, because He is an infinitely worthy Father! Christ obeyed the Father. He said, "I seek not mine own will, but the will of the Father who hath sent me" (John 5:30). In John 4:34 He says, "My food is to do the will of him that sent me." When He prayed to the Father in the Garden of Gethsemane, He said, "Father, if it be possible, let this cup pass from me; nevertheless, not as I will, but as thou wilt" (Matt. 26:39). If Christ could be subservient in His perfection, certainly we can be subservient in our imperfection.

(7) The source of wisdom

Since God is our Father, He is infinitely wiser than we are. Therefore, we should be submissive to His will because He knows what is best.

What does knowing that God is your Father do for you? It removes fear, provides hope, ends loneliness, does away with selfishness, provides heavenly resources, demands obedience, and declares His wisdom. To begin your prayers with "Our Father, who art in heaven" is to indicate your eagerness to come as a child to a loving Father and to receive all that His love can possibly give you.

Focusing on the Facts

1. What two spiritual activities should a believer never cease? What Scripture supports that (see p. 18)?
2. What are some of the postures that people in the Bible have used for prayer? Describe some of the different places that people in the Bible prayed (see p. 19).
3. Must prayer occur at a prescribed time? Explain (see pp. 19-20).
4. Describe some of the circumstances that people in the Bible were in when they prayed (see p. 20).
5. Explain the significance of Christ's words "after this manner, pray ye" in Matthew 6:9 (see pp. 20-21).
6. What did the Old Testament saints do when they began their prayers? Support your answer with Scripture (see pp. 21-22).
7. What perspective should we have when we pray (see pp. 21-22)?
8. What does every statement in the Disciples' Prayer focus on? Explain (see p. 22).
9. What do liberal theologians teach about the fatherhood of God? What is the correct teaching (see pp. 22-23)?
10. How did the Old Testament Jewish believers view the fatherhood of God (see p. 23)?
11. Discuss five elements that Jewish people of the Old Testament times saw in the fatherhood of God (see pp. 24-25).
12. What did Christ tell His Jewish audience in Matthew 7:7-11 (see p. 26)?
13. What did the term *Father* mean to the Pharisees and scribes of Christ's time (see p. 26)?
14. How did the Stoics and Epicureans view the gods of their societies (see p. 27)?
15. Give a modern-day perspective on God and life (see p. 27).
16. What is special about the term Christ used for the word *Father* in Matthew 6:9 (see p. 28)?
17. Discuss seven things that happen as a result of having God as our Father (see pp. 28-31).

Pondering the Principles

1. Prayer is communion with God, and it is to be a way of life for every believer. In 1 Thessalonians 5:17 the apostle Paul says, "Pray without ceasing." How often do you commune with God during the day, and how much of your life do you share with Him? Write down all the concerns, thoughts, and plans you have in your life right now. Do you talk with God about every one of those things in your prayers? Since God rules in our lives, we should entrust every matter to Him. Commit yourself to sharing every aspect of your life with God in prayer throughout the day. One benefit you'll receive from doing that is the sense of a deeper intimacy in your relationship with God.

2. Read Psalm 29:2; 95:6-7; and 99:9. What do those verses exhort us to do? The Old Testament saints began their prayers by worshiping God regardless of their circumstances. Why is it important to do that? What perspective will a person have during prayer when he does that? Meditate on Psalm 95-96, and observe how the Lord is worshiped in those chapters. Memorize at least one of the Scripture references listed above.

3. If you are a Christian, you are a child of God (John 1:12). You can use the word *Father* in speaking to God as a term of endearment (Rom. 8:15), and you always have the right to come into God's presence in prayer. Carefully read Exodus 3:1-5 and Isaiah 6:1-5. What attitude should we have when we pray to God? What does Hebrews 4:16 say we can receive when we come before God? Since God is holy, we should revere Him, and because He loves us, we can seek help in times of need. Keeping those things in mind will help you to maintain a proper perspective when you pray.

4. The Disciples' Prayer begins, "Our Father, who art in heaven." God has the supernatural domain at His disposal. What does that tell you in regard to your needs? What are we exhorted to do in Proverbs 3:5-6? Read Matthew 7:7-11. What specifically does verse 11 say God will do for you? How should knowing that affect your relationship with God?

3
The Priority of Prayer

Outline

Introduction
A. Prayers of Submission
B. Prayers of Selfishness

Review
I. God's Paternity (v. 9*a*)

Lesson
II. God's Priority (v. 9*b*)
   A. The Concept of God's Name
      1. According to the Hebrews
      2. According to the Bible
         a) The scriptural references
            (1) In the Old Testament
            (2) In the New Testament
         b) The specific titles
   B. The Consecration of God's Name
      1. The proper meaning
         a) *Hallowed* explained
            (1) To make an ordinary thing extraordinary
            (2) To treat someone or something as sacred
         b) *Hallowed* exemplified
            (1) The complaint
            (2) The command
            (3) The conduct
            (4) The consequence
      2. The protective measure
         a) The problem
         b) The protection
      3. The practical methods
         a) Believe that God exists
         b) Know the kind of God that He is
         c) Be constantly aware of His presence
         d) Live in obedience to Him

Introduction

Many people see prayer as a way of getting things from God. They think prayer is a means to an end—and that end is usually a selfish one. Someone said that men use prayers like sailors do pumps when a ship leaks. They use it as a spiritual parachute. They're glad it's there, and hope they'll never have to use it. People have developed a wrong perspective of prayer; they don't view it the same way God does. But the Disciples' Prayer in Matthew 6, which is a model for all prayers, indicates that prayer is not primarily for us but for God. The purpose of prayer is not for us to gain what we think we need; it's for God to have an opportunity to manifest His glory. If we never gain anything from prayer but the opportunity to commune with God, that should be sufficient for us.

A. Prayers of Submission

When you pray, you are entering into the very throne room of the living God of the universe and communing with Him. Picturing that in our minds should be enough to draw us to pray constantly. And prayer is more than just the privilege of communing with God; it's an opportunity for the Lord to display His glory. It is a vehicle by which He can demonstrate who He is. One saint said that true prayer brings the mind to the immediate contemplation of God's character and holds it there until the believer's soul is properly impressed. Prayer is to impress you with God more than it is to impress God with you or your needs. We shouldn't pray to tell God about our holiness or our needs but to allow God to be on display. In John 14:13 Jesus says, "Whatever ye shall ask in my name, that will I do, that the Father may be glorified in the Son." Why will God hear and answer your prayers? So He will be glorified.

Prayer is foremost a recognition of God's majestic glory and an act of submission to it. All our petitions, passions, requests, needs, trials, and problems are subject to God's name (Matt. 6:9), kingdom (v. 10), and will (v. 10). We see reference to God meeting our needs (v. 11), forgiving us (v. 12), and leading us (v. 13). But those three things happen only when God is given His proper place.

B. Prayers of Selfishness

True worship begins with forgetting self and glorifying God. Unfortunately, many people think of prayer as a way of bringing the Lord into line with their own desires. Today in the church, a prominent movement is encouraging people to claim certain things from God and tell Him He must do such-and-such for them. There are people who say that by faith, we can demand things from the Lord. I once heard someone say that if you're a spirit-filled Christian, you should never be ill, and thus you can demand that God keep you well. Whether we like to admit it or not, many of us make similar demands of God in our prayers.

The Old Testament has an example of selfish prayer. In Genesis 28:20-21 we read, "Jacob vowed a vow, saying, If God will be with me, and will keep me in his way that I go, and will give me bread to eat, and raiment to put on, so that I come again to my father's house in peace; then shall the Lord be my God." How is that for conditional prayer? Jacob was saying he would follow the Lord if He did certain things for him. Verse 22 continues, "This stone, which I have set for a pillar, shall be God's house: and of all that thou shalt give me I will surely give the tenth unto thee." Jacob said he would give money to God if God would do what was asked of Him. Jacob's vow was not spiritual; it was carnal. We should never demand anything from God in our prayers. Don't let someone say that if you have enough faith, God will give you what you want. That's playing games with God's sovereignty.

The purpose of prayer is to uplift God and manifest His majesty and sovereign will. Anything else in our prayers must be brought into subjection to that. The entire model of prayer Jesus gives us in Matthew 6:9-13 focuses on God. That's the matter Jesus was dealing with when He taught the prayer. The scribes and Pharisees had perverted prayer from what God intended it to be and made it into a traditional exercise used to draw attention to themselves. They used their prayers hypocritically to show how spiritual they were. They thought they needed to inform God of things He didn't know, and they used vain repetitions as pagans did in attempts to badger God into giving them what they wanted. Their prayers were illegitimate and nonscriptural. That's why in Matthew 6, Jesus says their giving, fasting, and praying is not according to God's standard. In verse 9 He says, "After this manner, therefore, pray ye." He told the Jewish religious leaders to stop being self-centered and to focus on God when they prayed.

Review

I. GOD'S PATERNITY (v. 9*a*; see pp. 22-31)

"Our Father, who art in heaven."

God is our Father. The Aramaic term Jesus uses in Matthew 6:9 is *Abba*. That is an intimate, warm, familial term. God is not a distant ogre or a capricious, immoral Being who steps on His subjects. He is a loving, tender, caring Father. At His disposal are all the treasures of heaven, which He makes available to the saints so His name may be glorified. God listens to our prayers because He cares for us. He will meet our needs because He has unlimited eternal resources. All prayer begins with the recognition that God is a loving Father. You don't have to badger Him into a response. The prophet Elijah taunted the prophets and priests of Baal because their god did not respond to them (1 Kings 18:27), but you don't have to worry about that. The Lord is waiting for you to enter His presence.

Christ began the Disciples' Prayer with the recognition that God is a loving Father who has the resources to meet our needs. For example, God said to Moses, "I know thee by name" (Ex. 33:17). Have you ever wondered why the Bible has so many genealogies? Why does God bother with all those names? He wants us to know that He cares for people and knows them by name. God is a loving Father who cares even about the little things.

Lesson

II. GOD'S PRIORITY (v. 9*b*)

"Hallowed be thy name."

The first request in the Disciples' Prayer is on God's behalf. The prayer doesn't begin by focusing on you. There are other requests in the prayer that focus on God: "thy kingdom come" and "thy will be done" (v. 10). Next we see requests made on our behalf: "Give us this day. . . . Forgive us our debts. . . . And lead us not into temptation" (vv. 11-13). The prayer concludes by focusing on God again: "For thine is the kingdom, and the power, and the glory, forever" (v. 13).

Prayer always begins with God's priorities. Arthur W. Pink said, "How clearly, then, is the fundamental duty in prayer here set forth: self and all its needs must be given a secondary place and the Lord freely accorded the preeminence in our thoughts, desires and supplications. This petition must take the precedence, for the glory of God's great name is the ultimate end of all things" (*An Exposition of the Sermon on the Mount* [Grand Rapids:

Baker, 1974], pp. 161-62). When we say "hallowed be thy name" we put God in His proper place. Even though He cares for our needs and has the heavenly resources to meet those needs, our prayers are to begin on God's behalf. "Hallowed be thy name" is a warning against self-seeking prayer.

You may have said or heard the phrase "hallowed be thy name" many times when you've gone through the Disciples' Prayer. But do you know what it means? What is implied when you say that? Some people think it's like saying "long live the king" or that it's an epithet attached to God's name to give homage. However, when Jesus said "hallowed be thy name" He was saying something rich in meaning; what He said completely encompassed God's nature and man's response to His nature. Christ wasn't just reciting some nice words about God. Instead, He opened a whole dimension of respect, reverence, glory, and worship for God.

A. The Concept of God's Name

The concept of the word *name* in Matthew 6:9 is not restricted to a title. Today, people have names that generally don't refer to any particular characteristic about them; their names are just titles. For example, the name *John* means "God's gracious gift," but there are many people with that name who don't even care about God.

1. According to the Hebrews

The Hebrews attached special significance to God's name. In fact, they considered it so sacred that they made sure they didn't say it. That's ironic because they dishonored Him, disobeyed His Word, and destroyed His truths. Yet they had made the letters of His name sacred.

In the Old Testament, you may have seen the word *Jehovah*. However, there is no such word in Hebrew. Where did it come from? The name of God in Exodus 3:14, where He says, "I Am That I Am," is *Yahweh*. Another name that was used for God is *Adonai*, which means "the Lord God." The Jews didn't want to use the word *Yahweh* because it was considered sacred. In fact, orthodox Jews would get very upset at you for saying that word. The Old Testament Jews, to avoid saying *Yahweh*, took the consonants from that name, the vowels from *Adonai*, came up with *Jehovah*, which is not a word. They made it up so they wouldn't have to say the real word used for God's name. However, that was a superficial act, for they constantly blasphemed God's person.

2. According to the Bible

The concept Christ was communicating in the phrase "hallowed be thy name" is that we respect God for who He is—not just His name. It's an all-encompassing concept. Let's examine what it meant to hallow someone's name in Bible times.

a) The scriptural references

(1) In the Old Testament

(*a*) 1 Samuel 18:30

Here, we read, "The princes of the Philistines went forth; and it came to pass, after they went forth, that David behaved himself more wisely than all the servants of Saul, so that his name was much esteemed." Because David acted more wisely than the other servants of Saul, he developed a good reputation with the Israelites. The end of the verse says, "His name was much esteemed." That doesn't mean the letters in his name were esteemed but that David himself was. Today people use the expression, "So-and-so has made a name for himself." In other words, there is something about that person's character that is worthy of our praise. So in the Bible, a person's name represented a person's character.

(*b*) Exodus 34:5-7

In Exodus 33, Moses has a discussion with God. He wanted to see the Lord's glory so he could make sure God was with him. In verse 18 he says, "I beseech thee, show me thy glory." Then in Exodus 34:5, we see God's response: "The Lord descended in the cloud, and stood with him there, and proclaimed the name of the Lord." When the Lord proclaimed His name, did He say, "Lord" over and over again? No. Verse 6 begins, "The Lord passed by before [Moses], and proclaimed." The proclamation in verse 6 is equivalent to the proclamation in verse 5; so verse 6 clarifies what it means to proclaim the name of the Lord. Verses 6-7 read, "The Lord passed by before [Moses], and proclaimed, The Lord, the Lord God, merciful and gracious, long-suffering, and abundant in goodness and truth, keeping mercy for thousands, forgiving iniquity and transgression and sin, and who will by no means clear the guilty, visiting the iniquity of the fathers upon the children [a reference to God's judgment]." So when God said, "Here is My name," He said, "I am merciful, gracious, long-suffering, abundant in goodness and truth, merciful, and forgiving." The name of God is the composite of all His attributes. Hallowing God's name does not mean having an aversion to speaking it out loud. It is hallowing all that He is in terms of His nature.

(c) Psalm 9:10

The psalmist wrote, "They who know thy name will put their trust in thee." If the word *name* is taken literally to mean God's name itself, we would be saying that everyone who knows the word *God* trusts in Him. However, that's not the case. An accurate rendition of Psalm 9:10 would be, "Those who perceive the fullness of who God is put their trust in Him." When a person comes to understand the Lord's character, he will trust Him.

(d) Psalm 7:17

King David said, "I will praise the Lord according to his righteousness, and will sing praise to the name of the Lord most high." The word *name* in that verse refers to all that God is.

(e) Psalm 102:15

Psalm 102:15 says, "The nations shall fear the name of the Lord, and all the kings of the earth thy glory." It's not the letters of God's name that the nations fear; it's the embodiment of all that God is.

(f) Psalm 113:1-5

The psalmist said, "Praise ye the Lord. Praise, O ye servants of the Lord, praise the name of the Lord. Blessed be the name of the Lord. . . . From the rising of the sun unto the going down of the same, the Lord's name is to be praised. The Lord is high above all nations, and his glory above the heavens. Who is like unto the Lord, our God, who dwelleth on high." All that God is, is cause for praising Him.

The concept of God's name referring to His attributes also appears in Isaiah 50:10; 56:6; 59:19; and Psalm 20:7.

(2) In the New Testament

A key verse for understanding that hallowing the Lord's name is the same thing as hallowing His attributes is John 17:6. Jesus said to the Father, "I have manifested thy name unto the men whom thou gavest me." What did He mean when He said, "I have manifested thy name"? Jesus had revealed who God was. John 1:14 says, "The Word was made flesh, and dwelt among us (and we beheld his glory, the glory as of the only begotten of the Father), full of grace and truth." Christ manifested God. He said to the disciple Philip, "He that hath seen me hath seen the Father" (John 14:9). Jesus is the manifestation of all that God is.

b) The specific titles

The various names of God that appear in the Bible express the different aspects of His character.

(1) *Elohim*—This Hebrew name for God appears in Genesis which says, "In the beginning God created the heaven and the earth." *Elohim* means "the Creator God." The Lord is to be hallowed as Creator. Eighteenth-century English hymn writer Isaac Watts said this in the hymn "I Sing the Mighty Power of God":

I sing the mighty pow'r of God,
That made the mountains rise,
That spread the flowing seas abroad
And built the lofty skies.

I sing the goodness of the Lord
That filled the earth with food;
He formed the creatures with His word
And then pronounced them good.

Lord, how Thy wonders are displayed
Where're I turn my eye:
If I survey the ground I tread
Or gaze upon the sky!

While all that borrows life from Thee
Is ever in Thy care,
And ev'rywhere that man can be,
Thou, God, art present there.

Everywhere, God is seen as the Creator.

(2) *El Elyon*—This name is used of God in Genesis
14:19, which says, "Blessed be Abram of the most
high God, possessor of heaven and earth." God
is the sovereign ruler over all the universe.

(3) *Jehovah-jireh*—the Lord will provide (Gen. 22:14)

(4) *Jehovah-nissi*—the Lord our banner (Ex. 17:15)

(5) *Jehovah-rapha*—the Lord that heals (Ex. 15:26)

(6) *Jehovah-shalom*—the Lord our peace (Judg. 6:24)

(7) *Jehovah-tsedeqenu*—the Lord our righteousness
(Jer. 23:6)

(8) *Jehovah-sabaoth*—the Lord of hosts (1 Sam. 1:3)

(9) *Jehovah-shammah*—the Lord is present (Ezek.
48:35)

(10) *Jehovah-meqadishkem*—the Lord who sanctifies
you (Ex. 31:13)

God's names all speak of His attributes; they show
the fullness of who He is. The greatest name ever
designated to Him is the name the Lord Jesus Christ,
which means "Lord, Savior, King." As the Lord Jesus
Christ, He drew to Himself many other names: the
Bread of Life (John 6:35), the Living Water (John

4:10-11; 7:37), the Way, the Truth, and the Life (John 14:6), the Resurrection (John 11:25), the Good Shepherd (John 10:11), the Branch (Isa. 4:2; 11:1; Zech. 6:12), the Bright and Morning Star (Rev. 22:16), and the Lamb of God (John 1:29, 36).

All the names of God reflect the characteristics of His majestic person. For example, Isaiah 9:6 says, "Unto us a child is born . . . and his name shall be called Wonderful, Counselor, The Mighty God, The Everlasting Father, The Prince of Peace." Those are designations of the Lord's nature. With that in mind, we can better understand verses such as Romans 1:5, which says, "We have received grace and apostleship, for obedience to the faith among all nations, for [the sake of] his name," or 3 John 7, which says, "For his name's sake they went forth." To hallow God's name is to perceive Him in the fullness of who He is.

B. The Consecration of God's Name

What does the word *hallow* mean? The first thing some people think of is Halloween. Others think of cloistered halls, ivy-covered walls, long robes, dismal chants, halos, musty churches, mournful music, and old religious traditions. Although the word *hallowed* is archaic, translators of the various versions of the Bible have kept it because of its familiarity. But many people don't know what it means.

1. The proper meaning

a) *Hallowed* explained

The word *hallowed* comes from the Greek verb *hagiazō*. The noun form of the word is *hagios*, which means "holy." When Christ said, "Hallowed be thy name" (Matt. 6:9), He was saying, "Holy be thy name." The word was never used in secular Greek, but it has two basic meanings in biblical Greek.

(1) To make an ordinary thing extraordinary

To hallow something is to make a common thing uncommon by bringing it into contact with something extraordinary. First Peter 1:16 reads, "Be ye holy." Before a person becomes a Christian, he is unholy; but he becomes holy when he comes into contact with God, who is holy. Is that the meaning used in Matthew 6:9? Are we making God holy through our prayers? No; He is already holy.

(2) To treat someone or something as sacred

To hallow something is also to treat it as sacred. This meaning appears more frequently in the Bible. To hallow God's name is to regard Him as holy. Saying "holy be Thy name" to God is not the same as saying "be ye holy" to a person. The latter refers to a person getting his life in line with God so that he will obtain the Lord's righteousness. But when you say to God "holy be Your name" you're saying, "May Your name be regarded and made manifest as holy." We don't make the Lord holy; we simply petition that He be revered as holy.

To be holy is to have a different quality of being. That's why God is called the Holy One—He is in a different sphere of life than we are. Exodus 20:8 says, "Remember the sabbath day, to keep it holy." In other words, the Sabbath day was to be different from all the other days. Leviticus 21:8 says that the Israelite priests were to be holy; they were to be different from other men and serve God. The word *holy* means "to be set apart." God lives in a different sphere; He is separated from us. He is holy and undefiled. Thus, according to the model prayer in Matthew 6, we are to speak to God with reverence in our prayers.

b) *Hallowed* exemplified

(1) The complaint

There is a good illustration in Numbers 20 that will help us understand what it means to hallow God's name. Verse 1 begins, "Then came the children of Israel, even the whole congregation, into the desert of Zin in the first month. . . . And there was no water for the congregation; and they gathered themselves together against Moses and against Aaron. And the people strove with Moses, and spoke, saying, Would God that we had died when our brethren died before the Lord! And why have ye brought up the congregation of the Lord into this wilderness, that we and our cattle should die there? And wherefore have ye made us to come out of Egypt, to bring us in unto this evil place? It is no place of seed, or of figs, or of vines, or of pomegranates; neither is there any water to drink" (vv. 1-5). The people of Israel complained to Moses and Aaron about lack of water.

(2) The command

The passage continues, "Moses and Aaron went from the presence of the assembly unto the door of the tabernacle of the congregation, and they fell upon their faces; and the glory of the Lord appeared unto them. And the Lord spoke unto Moses, saying, Take the rod, and gather thou the assembly together, thou, and Aaron, thy brother, and speak ye unto the rock before their eyes; and it shall give forth its water, and thou shalt bring forth to them water out of the rock: so thou shalt give the congregation and their beasts drink" (vv. 6-8). God told Moses, "Just speak to this rock, and I'll bring forth water."

(3) The conduct

Verses 9-11 say, "Moses took the rod from before the Lord, as he commanded him. And Moses and Aaron gathered the congregation together before the rock, and he said unto them, Hear now, ye rebels; must we fetch you water out of this rock? And Moses lifted up his hand, and with his rod he smote the rock twice." God told Moses to merely speak to the rock, but he hit the rock twice with a rod. He didn't do what God said.

(4) The consequence

After Moses struck the rock "water came out abundantly, and the congregation drank, and their beasts also. And the Lord spoke unto Moses and Aaron, Because ye believed me not, to sanctify me in the eyes of the children of Israel, therefore ye shall not bring this congregation into the land which I have given them" (vv. 11-12). (The word translated "sanctify" is *hagiazō* in the Septuagint, the Greek version of the Hebrew Old Testament. As we learned earlier, it means "revere," "honor," "glorify," or "set apart.") Apparently Moses didn't believe the rock would give water just by speaking to it, so he hit it twice with a rod. As a result, he never entered the Promised Land. Moses dishonored God before the Israelites by his action. By striking the rock, he probably thought the people would associate the miracle at least in part to him. He tried to steal some of the glory from God and was disobedient to Him. In his disbelief (v. 12) he failed to honor God.

2. The protective measure

   a) The problem

   To hallow God's name is to hold His matchless being in reverence and obey what He says. The phrase "hallowed be thy name" in Matthew 6:9 follows after the words "our Father," which protects us from becoming too sentimental about God as our daddy. Too many people today drag God down and make Him into a buddy. Some Christians talk to God on such a low level that they don't do justice to His hallowed name. They see God as a nice daddy who will give them everything.

   b) The protection

   The Jews took protective measures to avoid becoming overly sentimental toward God. They would've understood why Jesus said, "Our Father . . . hallowed be thy name" (Matt. 6:9). When they called God *Father*, they almost always added a title of reverence after that to balance their perspective toward the Lord. Their prayers would begin along these lines: "O Lord, Father and ruler of my Life" or, "O Father, King of great power, most high and almighty God." The Jews didn't want their concept of God as Father to keep them from also seeing Him as a sovereign, majestic king. They guarded carefully against sentimentalizing God.

   In his first epistle, Peter writes, "Sanctify [Gk., *hagiazō*] the Lord God in your hearts" (3:15). The Greek word *hagiazō* tells us we are to treat God as holy and give Him adoration and glory. To hallow something is to set it apart from everything common

45

and profane. We are to honor and adore the infinitely blessed true and only God. We cannot speak of Him in earthly terms; we are to address Him appropriately according to His power and holiness.

It's so easy for us to say "hallowed be thy name" without even thinking about what we're saying. We need to make sure we give God the place He deserves in our lives. Our hearts should long to glorify Him in every situation and relationship. In John 12:27-28, Jesus basically says, "Father, honor Your name in Me."

3. The practical methods

How can we make sure God's name is hallowed in our lives? Now I'm not just talking about making sure we don't use God's name in vain. Nor are we saying we should use the phrase "hallowed be thy name" whenever we worship the Lord or pray to Him. Let's look at some practical ways we can make sure God is hallowed in our lives.

a) Believe that God exists

We hallow God's name when we believe He exists. Hebrews 11:6 says, "He that cometh to God must believe that he is." You can never exalt the Lord unless you believe He exists. Interestingly, Scripture never tries to prove God's existence. That's because He is self-evident; He is axiomatic. An axiom is something that doesn't need to be proven. God is never proven, yet everything else is proven as it relates to God. The writers of Scripture never sought to prove the Lord's existence; they believed it. You'll never hallow God until you believe that He is. Astronomer Sir James Jeans said, "No astronomer can be an atheist." Immanuel Kant, a philosopher who had many strange views, was right when he said this: "The moral law within us and the starry heavens above us, drive us to God" (cited by William Barclay, *The Gospel of Matthew*, vol. 1 [Philadelphia: Westminster, 1975], p. 208). God is self-evident both in and around man. However there is more to hallowing God's name, for mere belief doesn't exalt Him.

b) Know the kind of God that He is

There are many people who say, "I believe in God," but they don't hallow His name because they don't have a proper perspective of Him. Knowing true doctrine about God and having true teaching from God will make a person revere God properly. Similarly, false doctrine about God and false teaching will make a person irreverent. Most people think that to take God's name in vain means to use the Lord's name with a swear word. However, you take His name in vain every time you have a thought about God that is not true of Him. When you doubt or question God, you take His name in vain. You can hallow His name only when you believe what is true about Him. The early church Father Origen said in his rebuttal to the Greek philosopher Celsus that the man who brings into his concept of God ideas that have no place there takes the name of the Lord God in vain (book 1, chapter 25).

Some people say that because God drowned the Pharaoh's army and wiped out the Canaanites, He is cruel. They say He is vindictive and harsh because He punished certain nations in the Old Testament. Even Job, while trying to figure out why things were going wrong for him, said to God, "Thou art become cruel to me" (30:21). People have accused God of being unloving and indiscriminately banishing people to an eternal hell. They see Him as an ally of Israel who goes around slaughtering other people whimsically. However, when you think any such wrong thoughts about God, you are not hallowing His name. John Wesley, after hearing a number of people criticize God, said that their god was his devil. Their thoughts of the true God were opposite what they should have been. To think of God unworthily is to be irreverent to His holy name.

It's possible for Christians to be irreverent not just by wrong thoughts but also by being ignorant of what is true about God. If you are ignorant about what God is like, then you will doubt Him when He does certain things in your life. You'll distrust Him and cause others to be repelled from Him. To hallow His name, you must believe that He is and you must

47

know what is true about Him. However, even when you do both, it's still possible not to hallow God.

c) Be constantly aware of His presence

We need daily to live our lives with the awareness that God is always in our presence; that helps us to make a priority of hallowing His name in every situation. In Psalm 16:8 David says, "I have set the Lord always before me." He was saying, "I see everything through God; He is my vision." To revere God is to live in the consciousness of His presence. Most of us think of God on an intermittent basis. Sometimes we'll think of Him a lot, and other times we won't. Some people think of the Lord for awhile right after a worship service is over, then they will go a whole week with very few thoughts about Him. But to really hallow His name is to draw conscious thoughts of Him into every thought, word, and action each day. Do you see God everywhere? Do you hallow His name in everything you do?

d) Live in obedience to Him

You cannot fully hallow God's name unless you obey Him. If you say, "Lord, I believe that You exist, that You are who the Bible says you are, and that You're always present in my life," but disobey Him, then you're not hallowing His name. The Disciples' Prayer doesn't just talk about God's name being hallowed in heaven or on earth; it talks about His name being hallowed in our lives. We should pray, "God, let me be a vehicle for Your holiness." Before you start asking the Lord for what you want, you should ask that your life be what it should be.

Martin Luther's larger catechism on this portion of the Lord's Prayer asks this question: "How is God's name hallowed amongst us?" His answer was, "When both our doctrine and our life are godly and Christian." When you have right thoughts about God and are obedient to Him, you are hallowing His name. So when we say "hallowed be thy name," we are saying, "God, manifest Your holiness by my right knowledge of who You are and my right living in response to it."

First Corinthians 10:31 says, "Whether, therefore, ye eat, or drink, or whatever ye do, do all to the glory of God." That's how we are to live. In Matthew 5:16 Jesus says, "Let your light so shine before men, that they may see your good works, and glorify your Father, who is in heaven." You will hallow God's name when He is on display in your life. Let the Lord's light shine through you so men will glorify Him.

How can we let God be manifest through our lives? By living in obedience to His Word. The Bible is clear about how we can glorify the Lord.

(1) By confessing Him as Lord (Phil. 2:9-11)

(2) By confessing sin (Josh. 7:19)

(3) By showing faith (Rom. 4:20)

(4) By bearing fruit (John 15:8)

(5) By praising Him (Ps. 50:23)

(6) By being content (2 Cor. 11:30)

(7) By proclaiming His truth (2 Thess. 3:1)

(8) By sharing God's Word (2 Cor. 4:5)

(9) By being sexually pure (1 Cor. 6:20)

(10) By being unified (Rom. 15:5-6)

In addition to the above, there are other ways we can demonstrate the majesty and glory of God in our lives. It's important that we manifest the Lord so others will learn the truth about Him and be drawn to Him.

Fourth-century bishop Gregory of Nyssa (a city in Asia Minor) prayed this: "May I become through thy help blameless, just and pious, may I abstain from every evil, speak the truth, and do justice. May I walk in the straight path, shining with temperance, adorned with incorruption, beautiful through wisdom and prudence. May I meditate upon the things that are above and despise what is earthly, showing the angelic way of life. . . . For a man can glorify God in no other way save by his virtue which bears witness that the Divine Power is the cause of his goodness." Is God's name hallowed in your life? That should be your first petition when you pray.

Focusing on the Facts

1. How do some people view prayer? Who is prayer primarily for (see p. 34)?
2. Why does God hear and answer our prayers (see p. 34)?
3. Why was Jacob's prayer in Genesis 28:20-21 selfish (see p. 35)?
4. What concept did the Hebrews have of God's name (see p. 36)?
5. What was Christ communicating by the phrase "hallowed be thy name" (Matt. 6:9; see p. 38)?
6. According to Exodus 34:5-7, what is the Lord's name (see pp. 38-39)?
7. The name of God is the _____ of all His _____ (see p. 39).
8. Explain what Christ means in John 17:6 when He says to the Father, "I have manifested thy name" (see p. 40).
9. What attributes of God are revealed in the names given to Him in the Old Testament (see pp. 40-41)?
10. As the Lord Jesus Christ, what names did God draw to Himself (see pp. 41-42)?
11. What two meanings does the word *hallowed* have? Which meaning is used in reference to God (see pp. 42-43)?
12. Keeping in mind the meaning of the word *hallowed* in reference to God, what does it mean when you say to God "holy be thy name" (see p. 43)?
13. How does Moses show irreverence for God's name in Numbers 20 (see pp. 43-45)?
14. Explain how the phrase "hallowed be thy name" balances out the address "our Father" (see p. 45).
15. What is the first thing we must do if we're to hallow God's name (see p. 46)?
16. How does our knowledge of God relate to hallowing His name? What does it mean to take the name of the Lord in vain (see p. 47)?
17. How can we make sure that we hallow God's name in our every thought, word, and action (see p. 48)?
18. You cannot fully _____ God's _____ unless you _____ Him (see p. 48).
19. Give some examples of how we can manifest God through our lives (see p. 49).

Pondering the Principles

1. Reread what Arthur W. Pink said about the priority of prayer on pages 36-37. Do you always begin your prayers on behalf of God and give Him preeminence in your thoughts and requests throughout your prayers? Why is it important for us to consider God first? How can you give God preeminence in your prayers

even while making requests? Write down some of the things you have said in your prayers in the past week, and see if some of those things would change in light of what you have just learned. Spend some time in prayer now, and lift those things up to the Lord, using the pattern for prayer that we have just discussed.

2. A good way to begin our prayers is by reciting God's attributes. What perspective will that give us? Explain two or three ways we can benefit from meditating on God's character when we pray. Think of several of God's attributes now, and explain how they should affect your prayers.

3. We hallow God's name when we bring honor and glory to it. In Matthew 5:16 Jesus says, "Let your light so shine before men, that they may see your good works, and glorify your Father, who is in heaven." Do your thoughts, words, and actions manifest God in your life? Do you think God is pleased with how you represent Him to the world? What aspects of your life do you need to work on to be a better representative for Him? What two or three good habits can you develop that will help you to bring glory to God's name daily in all that you do?

4
The Program of Prayer

Outline

Introduction
A. The Praise
B. The Promise
C The Program
D. The Preoccupation
   1.   With our will
   2.   With God's will
      a)   A personal priority
      b)   A prayerful perspective

Review
 I. God's Paternity (v. 9*a*)
II. God's Priority (v. 9*b*)

Lesson
III God's Program (v. 10*a*)
A. The Petitions
B. The Phrase
   1.   "Thy"
   2.   "Kingdom"
   3.   "Come"
C. The Probe
   1.   Whose is the kingdom?
      a)   It is God's kingdom
      b)   It is not a human kingdom
   2.   What is the kingdom?
      a)   The centrality
      b)   The chronology
      c)   The categories
         (1) The universal aspect
         (2) The earthly aspect
   3.   How will the kingdom come?

a)　By the conversion of unbelievers
　　　　(1)　It begins with an invitation
　　　　(2)　It includes repentance
　　　　(3)　It demands an act of the will
　　　　(4)　It is internal
　　b)　By the commitment of believers
　　c)　By the commencement of Christ's earthly rule

Introduction

Prayer is vital. It is to the Christian what breathing is to human life. It draws us into the presence of God and gives us life and sustenance. It's important to know how to pray. Yet Romans 8:26 says, "We know not what we should pray for as we ought." In the Disciples' Prayer in Matthew 6, Christ teaches us how to pray properly. His model prayer is not just something to be recited routinely; it is a skeleton for which all prayers are to find their form. The brief statements in the Lord's prayer open to us unlimited horizons for the content of our prayers.

The third phrase in the Disciples' Prayer is "thy kingdom come" (Matt. 6:10*a*). Let's look at the entire prayer to see how that phrase fits in the context: "Our Father, who art in heaven, hallowed be thy name. Thy kingdom come. Thy will be done in earth, as it is in heaven. Give us this day our daily bread. And forgive us our debts, as we forgive our debtors. And lead us not into temptation, but deliver us from evil. For thine is the kingdom, and the power, and the glory, forever. Amen" (Matt. 6:9-13).

As I approach the statement "thy kingdom come" I feel like a little boy standing on a beach with pail in hand, looking out over the vast sea. There is no way I can contain the sea in my bucket; likewise, there is no way I can articulate all that could be said about the phrase "thy kingdom come." We could spend all our lives examining what is contained in that statement. Only in eternity will we grasp all that it encompasses.

A.　The Praise

　　Eighteenth-century hymn writer Frances Havergal wrote these words to Christ in "His Coming to Glory":

> Oh the joy to see Thee reigning,
> Thee, my own beloved Lord!
> Every tongue Thy name confessing,
> Worship, honor, glory, blessing
> Brought to Thee with glad accord;
> Thee, my Master and my Friend,
> Vindicated and enthroned;
> Unto earth's remotest end
> Glorified, adored, and owned.

Those words capture the essence of the phrase "thy kingdom come." That phrase exalts Jesus Christ, recognizing that the One who has the right to reign over the earth is none other than Christ. He is the King of kings and Lord of lords (Rev. 19:16). When we pray "thy kingdom come" we are praying in accord with God's will, for Psalm 2:6-8 says, "Yet have I set my king upon my holy hill of Zion. I will declare the decree: The Lord hath said unto me, Thou art my Son; this day have I begotten thee. Ask of me, and I shall give thee the nations for thine inheritance, and the uttermost parts of the earth for thy possession." God wants to give the kingdoms of the world to His Son.

B. The Promise

In the Old Testament, God promised that someday His Son would reign on the throne of David. When David wanted to build a Temple for the Lord, God said through the prophet Nathan, "Thou shalt not build an house for my name, because thou hast been a man of war, and hast shed blood" (1 Chron. 28:3). Although God didn't allow David to build a Temple for Him, He did give him a great promise: "I will set up thy seed after thee . . . and I will establish his kingdom. He shall build an house for my name, and I will establish the throne of his kingdom forever" (2 Sam. 7:12-13). The Lord promised that someday a King—the eternal Son—would come and rule on David's throne forever. That promise appears throughout the Old Testament. Isaiah 9:6 says One would be born who would have the government upon His shoulders. He would be the Messiah. The word *messiah* means "anointed one, someone with a right to reign."

C. The Program

God's program centers on a person. History focuses on the One who will come again to reign as King of kings and Lord of lords (Rev. 19:16). Such was the hope of Israel, and such is the hope of the church and the world. The consummation of world history will occur when Jesus Christ reigns as King. Someone has well said that history is His story. History is the unfolding of God's redemptive plan in the person of Jesus Christ, and we are headed toward the time when Christ will rule. In Daniel 2:34-35 a statue representing the kingdoms of the world is smashed by a flying stone, which represents Christ. Then the stone fills the whole earth, which indicates Christ's complete rule over it. God does not have a program apart from a person. To pray "thy kingdom come" is to pray for Christ to reign.

D. The Preoccupation

A true child of God concerns himself not so much with his own plans as he does with the determinate plan of God revealed in the person of Jesus Christ. We are not to use prayer to inform God of our plans but to call on God to fulfill His own plans. A believer needs to come to the point where he says "thy kingdom come" instead of "my kingdom come." Although we may say "thy kingdom come" in our prayers, many of us fill our prayers with our own plans. Yet redemptive history—since the fall of man in Genesis, where we read that the seed of the woman will bruise the serpent's head (3:15)—is moving toward the glorification of the Son of God. The consummation of history will take place at the return of Christ.

1. With our will

We should be preoccupied with God's plan. However, that goes against our human nature. Have you noticed how much your prayers focus on yourself? We have a tendency to rush into God's presence and tell Him about our needs, plans, and concerns. We have a bent toward self. That is illustrated in the life of a baby. Babies know nothing of letting other people have their choice. They will scream when they want something. You can't say, "I'll get to you later; I have some other things to do right now." Babies are preoccupied with their needs. Toddlers show a bent toward self when they say, "That's mine! You can't have it."

As children grow up, the bent toward self continues. Through advertising and other means, junior high and high school children are told, "You are the king of your castle. You must determine your destiny. You are charting your own course and must govern your own life." The whole of human society is self-centered and thinks little of pronouns other than me, myself, and I.

The command that we are not to pray for our will but God's will goes against the grain of human nature. Some preachers today tell us we are to demand certain things from God. However, that comes from a total misunderstanding of God's plan in history, which is to glorify His name and carry out His will through His Son Jesus Christ. When a person genuinely confesses Christ as Lord and King of his life (Rom. 10:9), he affirms that the direction in his life is toward the exaltation of Jesus

Christ. Our causes are valid only when they are in harmony with the eternal causes of God. When we pray "thy kingdom come" we affirm that we are relinquishing the rule of our own lives and that we are letting the Holy Spirit take control to do whatever is necessary to bring God glory. However, that brings us into a confrontation with our human nature, which screams for its own will.

2. With God's will

a) A personal priority

When we preoccupy ourselves with the kingdom of God, we will value what should be valued—and no one will be able to take that away from us. People frequently ask me, "What will happen to America? Look at all the intrigues in our country. We are having economic, political, and educational problems. Look what's happening with humanism, immorality, and homosexuality. Will things get worse?" There are some pastors now on trial who could go to jail for their beliefs. There may be a time when we will not be allowed to say certain things, and will be put in jail for doing so. But if our causes are the same as God's, we will lose nothing. The investments we make into His kingdom cannot be touched.

I am grateful that God has made America my homeland, but my main concern is God's kingdom. I'm thankful for the freedoms we have in my country, but America is another passing nation in the history of the world. It will go the way of all the other nations that have existed. Inexorably built into this nation is the inevitable hour spoken of in God's Word: "Righteousness exalteth a nation, but sin is a reproach to any people" (Prov. 14:34). No nation ever lasts because built into it are the seeds of its own damnation, which is a result of sin's presence in the world. America has basically abandoned any godly causes. It has abandoned biblical standards and morality and is on its backside sliding downward. However, for Christians the issue isn't America or any other nation but the kingdom of God. If that's our concern then no one can touch what really matters to us.

Someone once asked me, "What would happen if you got persecuted for preaching?" That isn't something that could happen just in the future; many people in past generations and other countries have been persecuted for doing that. If I were put in jail for preaching, no one would be able to touch anything that is of value to me. People can take my car, house, clothes, and other possessions, but they can't take the love I have for my wife and children and their love for me. No one can take my love for other Christians or their love for me. No one can touch my friendships or my relationship with Christ. My investment in the kingdom is untouchable. That's where I invest my life. We should all be concerned with only those things that build up God's kingdom. Don't let the things of the world sidetrack you. Christians are to be committed to the kingdom, which will last forever. The gates of hell will never prevail against it (Matt. 16:18). Nations will come and go, including America.

b) A prayerful perspective

Do keep in mind that even though we are to be primarily concerned about God's kingdom, that doesn't mean we are to stop praying for our country's leaders. We should pray that our leaders will act, speak, and think in accord with God's principles. We are kingdom people and to pray for God's rule should be a basic part of our lives. We are to pray for God's causes. How can we say we have crowned Christ King of our lives when we are not preoccupied with His causes but our own?

In Matthew 6 the Lord presents a pattern for all prayer. In the context of the model prayer, He shows that the Jewish religious standards of His time were inadequate. Their motives for fasting and giving were not right, and their theology was inaccurate. Their relation to material things was not right, and their prayers were not right. According to Matthew 6:5, the Pharisees prayed to show off their supposed piousness. They prayed as hypocrites "standing in the synagogues and at the corners of the streets, that they may be seen by men." We should never pray with the idea of seeking our own gain. Rather, we are to pray "thy kingdom come." God's causes should be in our hearts.

Every part of the Disciples' Prayer speaks of God. Prayer is to focus on Him. In John 14:13 Jesus says, "Whatever ye shall ask in my name, that will I do, that the Father may be glorified in the Son."

Review

I. GOD'S PATERNITY (v. 9*a*; see pp. 22-31)

"Our Father, who art in heaven."

God is our loving Father. We can go to Him boldly without anxiety because we know He loves us.

II. GOD'S PRIORITY (v. 9*b*; see pp. 36-49)

"Hallowed be thy name."

God's name involves all that He is, and to hallow His name means to set it apart and glorify it. We hallow His name when we believe that He is, believe what is true about Him, acknowledge His continuous presence, and obey His Word.

Lesson

II. GOD'S PROGRAM (v. 10*a*)

"Thy kingdom come."

God's program is to exalt Christ. The consummation of history will occur when He reigns. The Talmud, which is the Jewish commentary on God's Word, says that the prayer in which there is no mention of the kingdom of God is not a prayer at all (*Berakoth* 21*a*). The kingdom is the issue; God has planned that Christ's kingdom will be established and that He will be the supreme Ruler. Consideration for God comes first in our prayers, not all our petitions. We are to begin our prayers by affirming our desire to see God's kingdom come and see God glorified. Any requests we make are legitimate only if they are in accord with God's purposes.

A. The Petitions

Why is it so hard to pray as we should? Looking at the logical order of the petitions in the Disciples' Prayer will help to answer that question. In verse 9 we read the first one: "Hallowed be thy name." We are to pray, "Lord, I want your name to be made holy in my life. I want to 'adorn the doctrine of God' (Titus 2:10). I want to live out the holiness that manifests You to the world." Yet as soon as we say we want to live for God, we face the reality that the kingdom of darkness exists in this world (Eph. 6:12). The kingdom of Satan withstands a believer's effort to live a hallowed life. That's why after we say "hallowed be thy name," we must

59

say "thy kingdom come" (Matt. 6:10). If Satan's kingdom is not withstood, God's name will not be hallowed. Unless we are transformed from the kingdom of darkness into the kingdom of Christ, we cannot hallow the Lord's name. Until Christ's reign is established, we have no capacity to hallow God.

The next petition in the Disciples' Prayer also appears in verse 10: "Thy will be done." God's kingdom cannot come unless His will is done, because His kingdom and will are one. Thus, we see a beautiful progression in Jesus' model prayer. God's will cannot be done until Christ is acknowledged as King, and no one will submit to His will until they first submit to His lordship. And unless a person makes Christ lord of his life, he has no capacity to hallow God's name. It's not enough to say "hallowed be thy name" unless we say "thy kingdom come." And we can't say "thy kingdom come" apart from saying "thy will be done." Christ will have the right to rule when His kingdom comes. That will give Him the privilege of expressing His will, which we must submit to.

B. The Phrase

Let's take a closer look at the phrase "thy kingdom come" by examining the words in the phrase.

1. "Thy"

This word is the pronoun *sou* in the Greek text.

2. "Kingdom"

The Greek word for "kingdom" is *basileia*. It means "rule" or "reign." I wish that everywhere the Greek word *basileia* appeared in the Greek text it had been translated "reign" instead of "kingdom." When we hear or see the word *kingdom*, we tend to think of kings, castles, forts, and knights. Some people might think of the Magic Kingdom of Disneyland, or of Sleeping Beauty. The word *kingdom* conjures thoughts of large estates, people riding horses, pomp and ceremony, maidens, moats, and strict laws.

When Pontius Pilate asked Jesus, "Art thou the King of the Jews?" (John 18:33), he was implicitly saying, "What kind of a king are You?" The world's concept of a king didn't fit Christ. Jesus answered Pilate by saying, "My kingdom is not of this world" (v. 36). By replacing the word *kingdom* with the word *reign*, we would have "thy reign come." That makes the petition clearer. Christ's kingdom won't have castles, moats, knights, fair maidens, and fancy crowns. We are to pray for Christ's sovereign rule.

3. "Come"

The word *come* in the Greek text is the verb *elthatō*. That's an aorist active imperative form of *erchomai*, which means "to suddenly come." Christ's kingdom won't progressively ooze its way into the world. It won't come gradually until one day we wake up and the kingdom is here; that's a postmillennial perspective. The verb form of the word *come* indicates that His kingdom will come suddenly and completely.

C. The Probe

The three words in the petition "thy kingdom come" raise three important questions we should think about.

1. Whose is the kingdom?

   a) It is God's kingdom

   When we say "thy kingdom come," whom does the word *thy* refer to? The antecedent is in verse 9: "Our Father." Whose kingdom are we praying for? God's. We're not talking about an earthly kingdom. We are not of this world (John 17:14). Our citizenship is not here; we are sojourners (Phil. 3:20; 1 Pet. 1:17). We look for a city whose builder is God (Heb. 11:10).

   b) It is not a human kingdom

   God's kingdom is unique; it's not like a man-made kingdom. Human kingdoms come and go. Egypt, Syria, Assyria, Babylon, Medo-Persia, Rome, and Greece are no longer world powers. Alexander the Great conquered everything from Europe down into Egypt and over into India, but nothing is left of that great empire. Historians say that at least twenty-one great civilizations have become extinct.

   In Daniel 5:26-28, Daniel tells the king of Babylon something that could be said in reference to all the nations of the world: "God hath numbered thy kingdom, and finished it. . . . Thou art weighed in the balances, and art found wanting. . . . Thy kingdom is divided." That night, the Medes and the Persians wiped out the Babylonian Empire.

All kingdoms go the way of all flesh. The descending power of sin causes inevitable decay and destruction. America will eventually fall to the wayside. Yet that will never happen to the church. You can't equate the kingdom of God with America. God's kingdom is different from a nation. I love the United States because it's my home, and we have great freedom here. There are people here who I love and who I wish knew Christ. But God's kingdom is to be my main concern. The Lord will tolerate this country as long as it is in accord with the cause of His kingdom. When that ceases to be so, it will pass away.

The focal point of our prayers is to be God's kingdom, not our own. We have to learn that our causes are not to take precedence in our prayers. In Matthew 6:33 the Lord says, "Seek ye first the kingdom of God, and his righteousness, and all these things shall be added unto you." He will take care of our needs—clothing, shelter, and food—when we seek His kingdom. We are to pray, "Lord, do whatever will advance Your kingdom and bring about Your reign."

2. What is the kingdom?

   a) The centrality

   What is the reign of Christ? What is the kingdom? The phrases "the kingdom of heaven" and "the kingdom of God" were frequently used by Jesus. He talked about the kingdom when He preached the good news. In Matthew 4:17 He says, "Repent; for the kingdom of heaven is at hand." Luke 4:43 reads, "I must preach the kingdom of God to other cities also; for therefore am I sent." The kingdom is the heart of Christ's message. Why is that? Because it's the heart of history. The reign of Christ is the apex of human history. Anything that does not come into accord with that does not matter. Jesus spent three years with the disciples teaching them about the kingdom. After He died and rose again, He appeared to His disciples over a period of forty days giving them commandments pertaining to the kingdom of God (Acts 1:2-3).

   b) The chronology

   Christ spoke frequently of His kingdom, and He spoke of it in terms of the past, present, and future

He indicated that His kingdom already existed because it embodied Abraham, Isaac, and Jacob (Matt. 8:11). He states that the kingdom is already here in Luke 17:21: "The kingdom of God is in the midst of you." The future aspect of the kingdom is spoken of in the Disciples' Prayer by the words "thy kingdom come" (Matt. 6:10a).

How can the kingdom already be here, yet need to come in the future? What is this kingdom that is past, present, and future all at the same time? The Jews thought God would establish a political kingdom. They believed the Messiah would come to conquer the Romans. However, that wasn't God's plan. In John 18:36 Jesus says, "My kingdom is not of this world." When the Jewish religious leaders told Pilate that Jesus claimed to be a king, Pilate didn't understand. He said in effect, "How can You claim to be a king?" When Christ was nailed to the cross, a sign was put above Him, and on it was written, "JESUS OF NAZARETH, THE KING OF THE JEWS" (John 19:19). It implied mockingly, "What kind of king is this?" People didn't understand because Christ's kingdom is not of this world.

c) The categories

If Christ's kingdom is not of this world, then what kind of a kingdom is it? And how can it be here, yet still lie in the future? To answer those questions, we must look at the two aspects of the kingdom: the universal aspect and the earthly aspect.

(1) The universal aspect

God is the King of the universe. There is no question about that. He made it, He maintains it, and He will bring it to its consummation. The psalmist wrote, "The Lord . . . ruleth over all" (Ps. 103:19). Jeremiah 10:10 reads, "The Lord is the true God . . . and an everlasting king." Psalm 29:10 says, "The Lord sitteth King forever." First Chronicles 29:11-12 sums up God's universal kingdom with these words: "Thine, O Lord, is the greatness, and the power, and the glory, and the victory, and the majesty; for all that is in the heaven and in the earth is thine. Thine is the kingdom, O Lord, and thou art exalted as head above all. . . . Thou reignest over all."

God is the universal King, and He mediates His rulership through His Son, by whom He made the world, and of whom is said, "He is before all things, and by him all things consist" (Col. 1:17). Paul said to Timothy that Christ is "the King eternal . . . the only wise God" (1 Tim. 1:17). God is the King of the universe, and He mediates His kingship through His Son, who is given the right to judge and reign.

(2) The earthly aspect

When Jesus said "thy kingdom come" (Matt. 6:10a) in model prayer, He was saying, "May the universal kingdom established in heaven come to earth." Notice the last words in Matthew 6:10: "In earth as it is in heaven." That is a typical Hebrew parallelism, and it can relate to the first three petitions in the Disciples' Prayer. We could say, "Thy kingdom come on earth as it is in heaven. Thy will be done on earth as it is in heaven. Hallowed be Thy name on earth as it is in heaven." Why? Because God's kingdom is established in heaven, His will is done there, and His name is hallowed there. So when we say "thy kingdom come," we are saying, "Lord, let the universal kingdom established in heaven come to earth."

God's name is not always hallowed on earth, His will is not always done, and His kingdom is not completely established because there is rebellion here. The Disciples' Prayer calls for God to bring His kingdom to earth and do away with sin and rebellion. Someday His kingdom will come, His name will be hallowed, and His will is going to be done. Eventually there won't be any distinction between His universal and earthly kingdoms. They will become one in His eternal reign. According to the Disciples' Prayer, we are to pray for Christ's rule on earth.

The world needs the rule of Jesus Christ. There is coming a day when He will reign with a rod of iron (Rev. 19:15). Our prayers for His rule to be established on earth will be answered. Revelation 20 speaks of the thousand-year reign of Christ here on earth. Then we will move into the eternal state where the earthly and universal kingdoms become one, and Christ will rule.

3. How will the kingdom come?

The best way to translate the phrase "thy kingdom come" is, "Let Your kingdom come, and let it come now." How do we bring God's kingdom to earth? How can this prayer be answered? There are three ways.

a) By the conversion of unbelievers

"Thy kingdom come" is an evangelistic prayer. His kingdom comes to earth in the lives of those who receive Him as Lord. Christ reigns in my life, and He should reign in yours. In that sense, He has brought His rule to this earth. In Luke 17 Jesus says, "The kingdom of God cometh not with observation. Neither shall [people] say, Lo here! Or, lo there! For behold, the kingdom of God is in the midst of you" (vv. 20-21). Apparently people were asking Him where the kingdom was. He said it was in their midst. He stood right before them, yet they didn't even recognize Him. Christ is the kingdom; you can't separate the kingdom from Him.

Christ's rule in our lives brings His reign to this earth. He mediates His kingdom through believers. That's why the Bible says that we are kings and priests (Rev. 1:6). So to say "thy kingdom come" is to pray that He take up His reigning residence in the lives of those who still rebel against Him. It's a prayer for salvation. You are Christ's castle on earth. The petition "thy kingdom come" calls for the conversion of men. The reason we should evangelize the lost is not as much for their sake as for Christ's. It's wrong for a person not to allow Christ to reign, because He is worthy of such a position. In Romans 1:5 Paul says that he preached "for obedience to the faith among all nations, for [the sake of] his name." Third John 7 says that for the Lord's sake, certain believers went forth to evangelize. The reason for becoming a Christian is to glorify God's name and kingdom.

What is involved in conversion?

(1) It begins with an invitation

In Matthew 22 Jesus illustrates the kingdom of heaven as a man having a big wedding banquet and sending out invitations to the guests. When those who were invited refused to come, the man said, "Go, therefore, into the highways, and as many as ye shall find, bid to the marriage" (v. 9). Likewise, Christ has invited people to come into His kingdom. To pray "thy kingdom come" is to pray an evangelistic, missionary prayer.

(2) It includes repentance

In Matthew 4:17 Jesus says, "Repent; for the kingdom of heaven is at hand." Mark 1:14-15 reads, "Jesus came into Galilee, preaching the gospel of the kingdom of God, and saying, The time is fulfilled, and the kingdom of God is at hand; repent, and believe the gospel." In a sense, the kingdom comes when a person repents. The invitation into the kingdom demands repentance.

(3) It demands an act of the will

Jesus tells a wise scribe in Mark 12:34, "Thou art not far from the kingdom of God." What did He mean by that? He was saying, "You've got the information necessary for getting into the kingdom; you just haven't made a decision to act on it." In Luke 9:62 He says, "No man, having put his hand to the plough, and looking back, is fit for the kingdom of God." You can know about the kingdom, but until you make a complete commitment to it, Christ's rule is not established in your heart.

(4) It is internal

Our Lord says in John 18:36, "My kingdom is not of this world." His kingdom is internal; it is of the heart. It is entered by repentance and commitment and is offered to every man.

How Should We Respond to Christ's Invitation?

1. Seek the kingdom

Jesus said, "Seek ye first the kingdom of God, and his righteousness" (Matt. 6:33). You should seek God's kingdom. If there is an opportunity for Christ to reign, you should look for it with all your heart. Luke 16:16 says, "The law and the prophets were until John [the Baptist]; since that time the kingdom of God is preached, and every man passeth into it." The word translated "presseth" is the verb *biazetai* in the Greek text, which means "to enter violently." When a person with a right heart sees the kingdom, he hurries into it. He sees the value of God's kingdom and rushes to grasp it. Is that your attitude? We should pray "thy kingdom come" with the hope that men will rush to have Christ reign in their lives.

2. Value the kingdom

    In Matthew 13:44 Jesus says, "The kingdom of heaven is like [a] treasure." In verses 45-46, He says the kingdom of heaven is like a "pearl of great price." It's of inestimable value. Because it's worth so much, we should run to grasp it.

3. Receive the kingdom

    We are to take hold of the kingdom by faith. Lip service won't suffice. Matthew 7:21 says, "Not every one that saith unto [Christ], Lord, Lord, shall enter into the kingdom of heaven." Money can't get a person into the kingdom. It's easier for a camel to go through the eye of a needle than for a rich man to enter heaven (Matt. 19:24). Self-righteousness doesn't quality a person, for Matthew 5:20 says, "Except your righteousness shall exceed the righteousness of the scribes and Pharisees, ye shall in no case enter into the kingdom of heaven." How can you enter? By faith (Eph. 2:8-9). Receive Christ's invitation, repent of your sin, and affirm the lordship of Christ. When you do that, an internal miracle will take place. You have to seek the kingdom with all your heart and realize its value.

   b) By the commitment of believers

    You may say, "I'm already a Christian. I pray for God's reign in the world, and for unbelievers to open their hearts to His rule." You may have the same attitude as nineteenth-century English missionary Henry Martyn, who once ran out of a temple in India and said, "I cannot endure existence if Jesus is to be so dishonored!" How does the phrase "thy kingdom come" apply to those of us who already have Christ reigning in our hearts?

If you are a Christian, it's true that the Lord's kingdom is already in your heart. Christ is ruling in you. However, it's important for us to daily affirm that we bow our knee to that rule. We must be committed to Christ's authority and confess that He is Lord. We frequently come to crossroads in our lives where we need to choose between doing God's will or our will. Thus, we need to affirm our commitment to God's causes. Since Christ is Lord, we need to submit to His lordship. That involves responding to the royalty residing in us.

In Romans 14:17 Paul says, "The kingdom of God is not food and drink, but righteousness, and peace, and joy in the Holy Spirit." The kingdom is not external; it is righteousness, peace, and joy. If you want Christ's kingdom to come in your life, you should pray, "Lord, make me more righteous. Fill me with Your blessed peace. May I know the fullness of the joy of the Holy Spirit." When you give yourself over to the virtues that the Spirit wants to produce in your life, Christ's reign will be made manifest in you.

c)   By the commencement of Christ's earthly rule

Someday, the heavens will split wide open, and Jesus will descend onto the Mount of Olives to establish His kingdom (Zech. 14:4). He will have a thousand-year reign (Rev. 20:4) and will rule with a rod of iron (Rev. 19:15). At that time, the prayer "thy kingdom come" will be answered. The universal kingdom will become established as an earthly kingdom. Christ will reign in righteousness, justice, truth, and peace. At the end of the thousand years, the earthly kingdom will merge into the universal kingdom, and never again will there be a distinction. The curse will be reversed, and everything will be as God meant it to be before the Fall of man.

Israel and the church have prayed a long time for God's kingdom to come. In Acts 1:6, the disciples ask Jesus, "Lord, wilt thou at this time restore again the kingdom to Israel?" The Lord answered, "It is not for you to know the times or the seasons, which the Father hath put in his own power" (v. 7). Jesus will come to set up His kingdom, and we are to remain busy until then. It's destined that Christ will rule this earth on the throne of David in the city of Jerusalem and reverse the curse that has been brought to this earth. Like Peter, we should be "looking for and hasting unto the coming of the day of God" (2 Pet. 3:12).

When we pray "thy kingdom come," we are praying that Christ's reign will come in the lives of people who don't know Him, that His reign will be expressed in our lives to the fullness He is worthy of, and that someday He will return to earth to break the tyranny of sin. Because the verb form of the word translated "come" refers to instantaneous action, we are praying for Christ's reign to be expressed immediately in believers, unbelievers, and on the earth. The glorious day is coming when Christ will rule the world. In the meantime, the kingdom is in our midst as He rules in our hearts.

Focusing on the Facts

1. What Old Testament promise did God give regarding His Son? Support your answer with Scripture (see p. 55).
2. What is to be our main preoccupation in prayer (see p. 56)?
3. Why is it difficult for us to be preoccupied with God's plan (see p. 56)?
4. Our causes are valid only when they are in _____ with the _____ _____ of God (see p. 57).
5. Give examples of some of the things people will never be able to take away from us. What does that tell us about where we should invest our lives (see p. 58)?
6. How should we pray for our country's leaders (see p. 58)?
7. What is God's program? How should that affect our prayers (see p. 59)?
8. Why is it hard for us to live out the holiness that manifests God to the world (see pp. 59-60)?
9. What do people usually think of when they hear or read the word *kingdom*? What is another word we can use to clarify the petition "thy kingdom come" (see p. 60)?
10. How will Christ's kingdom come (see p. 61)?
11. In what way is God's kingdom different from human kingdoms (see pp. 61-62)?
12. How do we know that the kingdom of heaven was a central theme in Christ's life? Support your answer with Scripture (see p. 62).
13. Explain the past, present, and future aspects to God's kingdom (see pp. 62-63).
14. What does Scripture say about God's universal rule (see pp. 63-64)?

15. Why can "thy kingdom come" be considered an evangelistic prayer (see p. 65)?
16. Described what is involved in conversion (see p. 66).
17. What did Christ liken the value of the kingdom to (Matt. 13:44-45)? How can a person enter the kingdom (see p. 67)?
18. If Christ is already reigning in your heart, how does the prayer "thy kingdom come" apply to you (see pp. 67-68)?
19. How will Christ's kingdom come in the fullest sense (see p. 68)?
20. What perspective should we have regarding Christ's coming kingdom (2 Pet. 3:12; see p. 69)?

Pondering the Principles

1. Frequently when we ask God to help us live in a Christlike manner, we run into opposition from the kingdom of darkness. Although Christ's kingdom is in the heart of every Christian, we need to make a commitment to keeping our will in accord with God's will. Ephesians 4:17-32 has some words concerning the difference between those who live as children of darkness and those who live as children of light. Verses 25-32 specify how Christians should live. Look over those verses, and think of some practical ways to apply those commands to your life. By knowing how to act when confronted with a choice between obeying or disobeying God's will, you will be prepared to resist Satan and consequently hallow God's name.

2. What does God desire according to 2 Peter 3:9? What are we commanded to do in 1 Timothy 2:1? One aspect of praying for Christ's kingdom to come to earth is praying for the salvation of unbelievers. Are you actively praying for the salvation of your unsaved relatives or friends? What other actions could you take that might help lead to their salvation?

3. We have much to look forward to in the coming earthly reign of Jesus Christ. First Peter 1:4 says we have "an inheritance incorruptible, and undefiled, and that fadeth not away, reserved in heaven for [us]." Carefully read Revelation 21 and 22. As you read, think of what eternity will be like with Christ. What aspects of eternity do you especially look forward to? Do you pray with anticipation for the coming of Christ's eternal kingdom? How can we benefit from having such a perspective? Take some time now to pray to the Lord and praise Him for the wonderful future set before us.

5
The Plan of Prayer—Part 1

Outline

Introduction
A. The Power of Prayer
   1. The examples
   2. The exhortations
B. The Paradox of Prayer
   1. The dilemma
   2. The danger
C. The Pattern of Prayer

Review
   I. God's Paternity (v. 9a)
  II. God's Priority (v. 9b)
 III. God's Program (v. 10a)

Lesson
IV. God's Plan (v. 10b)
   A. The Negative Perspective
      1. Examining the negative viewpoints
         a) Praying with bitter resentment
         b) Praying with passive resignation
            (1) Explaining passive resignation
            (2) Exemplifying passive resignation
            (3) Eliminating passive resignation
                (a) Considering the framework of God's will
                (b) Considering the freedom of man's choice
                (c) Praying with theological reservation
      2. Eradicating the negative viewpoints
         a) The parable of persistence
         b) The principle of persistence
         c) The practice of persistence

Introduction

A. The Power of Prayer

1. The examples

   The Bible teaches us that prayer can make a difference. It can be very effective. For example, when Abraham's servant prayed for a wife for Isaac, Rebekah appeared (Gen. 24:12-15). Jacob wrestled, prayed, and prevailed with the angel of the Lord (Christ) and afterwards, Esau's mind was turned from twenty years of revenge (Gen. 32:24—33:15). Joshua prayed about Israel's defeat in battle at Ai, and Achan's sin was discovered (Josh. 7). Hannah prayed, and Samuel was born (1 Sam. 1:9-20). David prayed that Ahithophel's counsel would be turned into foolishness (2 Sam. 15:31). When his counsel was not followed, Ahithophel hung himself (2 Sam. 17:23). King Asa prayed, and victory was won (2 Chron. 14:11-12).

   King Jehoshaphat prayed, and God turned away his enemies (2 Chron. 20:6-27). Isaiah and Hezekiah prayed, and in twelve hours, 185,000 Assyrians were slain (Isa. 37:15-38). Mordecai and Esther fasted and prayed, and Haman's plot to destroy the Jewish people was thwarted. The king had Haman hanged on his own gallows (Esther 4:15-16; 7:10). Ezra prayed at Ahava, and God protected the Israelites from their enemies (Ezra 8:21-23). Nehemiah prayed that he might restore Jerusalem, and King Artaxerxes granted permission (Neh. 1-2). Elijah prayed, and there were three-and-one-half years of drought (James 5:17). Then he prayed again, and there was rain (James 5:18). Elisha prayed, and a child was raised from the dead (2 Kings 4:32-35). Believers in the early church prayed, and Peter was released from jail (Acts 12:5-11). Scripture records that prayer is effective.

2. The exhortations

   God's Word specifically states that prayer is effective. James 5:16 says, "The effectual, fervent prayer of a righteous man availeth much." The context of the verse clarifies that statement. Verses 14-15 say, "Is any sick among you? Let him call for the elders of the church; and let them pray over him, anointing him with oil in the name of the Lord; and the prayer of faith shall save the sick, and the Lord shall raise him up; and if he have committed sins, they shall be forgiven him." When a person's sin causes an illness and God is besought in a prayer of confession on behalf of a penitent individual, that prayer is effective.

An illustration of effectual prayer is given in James 5:17-18: "Elijah was a man subject to like passions as we are, and he prayed earnestly that it might not rain; and it rained not on the earth by the space of three years and six months. And he prayed again, and the heaven gave rain; and the earth brought forth her fruit." You may think that the prayer was effective because a great man like Elijah offered it. But James said Elijah "was a man subject to like passions as we are" (v. 17). He was a man like us. Since God answered Elijah's prayer, He will also answer our prayers. We won't be able to pray the same way as Elijah did because he received special revelation from God concerning His will, but if we are in agreement with God's will, He is going to respond.

Jesus said, "Men ought always to pray, and not to faint" (Luke 18:1). In 1 Thessalonians 5:17 Paul says, "Pray without ceasing." He also said we are to pray "always with all prayer and supplication" (Eph. 6:18).

B. The Paradox of Prayer

1. The dilemma

God answers prayer specifically and directly. Now that brings up a very interesting issue: Do we really need to say, "God, Your will be done"? Won't God do what He wants to anyway because He is sovereign? Some people have taken this issue so far that they question the validity of prayer. They say, "Isn't God in charge of everything? If He does everything according to His plan, then why should we pray for His will to be done?" Then comes this question: Does God ever change His mind? Does prayer help make God do something other than what He had planned to do? If we are persistent enough, will God let us have our way and override His will? Does the Lord have to answer our prayers at all?

The questions people have about the relationship between prayer and God's will could be summed up into two questions: If God is sovereign, why pray? If prayer is commanded, then how can God be sovereign? I believe there are answers to those questions, but I don't know what they are. I believe that prayer as it relates to God's will is one of the great pardoxes of Scripture. God's mind is infinite compared to our minds, and the paradox poses an impossible dilemma for us. The majesty and infinite knowledge of the Lord is demonstrated to us in that we cannot resolve that apparent contradiction—which is not a contradiction at all in God's mind.

Perplexing Paradoxes in the Bible

There are other paradoxes in Scripture that cannot be fully explained:

1. Who wrote Matthew's gospel?

    People will give two answers to that: Some will say Matthew, and others will say the Holy Spirit. Did Matthew write one verse and the Holy Spirit write the next? No; they didn't alternate verses or chapters. Was Matthew just a robot through whom the Holy Spirit dictated? No; because Matthew's heart, feelings, and vocabulary are evident in his gospel. Matthew and the Holy Spirit were both completely involved. We cannot conceive of 200 percent of something, yet that reminds us of where we are in comparison to God.

2. Who lives your Christian life?

    You might quote Galatians 2:20, where Paul says, "I live; yet not I, but Christ liveth in me." But Paul also said, "I keep under my body, and bring it into subjection" (1 Cor. 9:27). Is Christ living your Christian life, or are you? Both of you are. You present your body as a living sacrifice (Rom. 12:1), and Christ lives in you. How can it be 100 percent you *and* 100 percent Christ? It's beyond our reasoning, but again that proves God is infinitely beyond us.

3. Was Christ God or man?

    He was both. That's like asking if it's colder in the mountains or in the winter. Christ was 100 percent God and 100 percent man. However, our minds cannot conceive of 200 percent of something. To us, that's a paradox.

4. How did you become a Christian?

    Some will say that God chose us before the foundation of the world (Eph. 1:4). It was predetermined. He wrote our names in the Lamb's Book of Life. Others will emphasize that they chose to receive Christ into their lives. Both answers are right. A person must receive Christ, and he is sovereignly chosen by God. Yet in our minds, we can't put the two together.

2. The danger

   When you find a paradox in Scripture, don't try to come up with an answer that fits in the middle and ruin the seemingly paradoxical facts. Some of us are tempted to do that. On the issue of salvation one man said, "God throws one vote for you, the devil throws one vote against you, and you cast the deciding vote." That's not true. Don't try to find a middle ground for paradoxes in the Bible; let them exist as they are.

God is sovereign. He has predetermined the flow of the universe. He knows the end from the beginning and will do what He plans to do. On the other hand, prayer works. Don't worry about trying to figure out exactly how those truths fit together; you'll just destroy your prayer life doing that. You might end up thinking that God is going to do everything His way, so there's no use in praying. Such an attitude disregards Scripture's command to pray.

C. The Pattern of Prayer

The Disciples' Prayer is not a prayer to be ritualistically spoken every Sunday morning. Rather, it is a pattern for all prayer. The last thing God wants anyone to do is routinely recite it. Prayer must flow from a truly committed heart. It ought to define your spirit, your attitude toward God.

Prayer is to be said with different words centered on the same thoughts. An unknown author put it this way:

I cannot say "our" if I live only for myself in a spiritual, watertight compartment.

I cannot say "Father" if I do not endeavor each day to act like His child.

I cannot say "who art in heaven" if I am laying up no treasure there.

I cannot say "hallowed be thy name" if I am not striving for holiness.

I cannot say "thy kingdom come" if I am not doing all in my power to hasten that wonderful day.

I cannot say "thy will be done" if I am disobedient to His Word.

I cannot say "in earth as it is in heaven" if I will not serve Him here and now.

I cannot say "give us . . . our daily bread" if I am dishonest or an "under the counter" shopper.

I cannot say "forgive us our debts" if I harbor a grudge against anyone.

I cannot say "lead us not into temptation" if I deliberately place myself in its path.

I cannot say "deliver us from evil" if I do not put on the whole armor of God.

I cannot say "thine is the kingdom" if I do not give to the King the loyalty due Him as a faithful subject.

I cannot attribute to Him "the power" if I fear what men may do.

I cannot ascribe to Him "the glory" if I am seeking honor only for myself.

I cannot say "forever" if the horizon of my life is bounded completely by the things of time.

Prayer is to express what's in our hearts, and the Disciples' Prayer is a pattern that should be present in all our prayers.

Review

I. GOD'S PATERNITY (v. 9a; see pp. 22-31)

"Our Father, who art in heaven."

We recognize at the beginning of our prayers that God is a loving Father. We are not coming into the presence of a dragon or some evil deity. There is no need for us to cower in fear of what He might do to us. God is our loving Father, and He seeks the best for us. Because He is in heaven, He has at His disposal all the resources of eternity with which to meet our needs.

II. GOD'S PRIORITY (v. 9b; see pp. 36-49)

"Hallowed be thy name."

"Hallowed be thy name" is the first petition in the prayer. We are to seek that God's name be honored through our lives.

III. GOD'S PROGRAM (v. 10a; see pp. 59-69)

"Thy kingdom come."

We should look forward to Christ's earthly reign. There are three ways that Christ's rule can be expressed on earth: Through the conversion of unbelievers, through the commitment of believers, and when Christ returns to establish His millennial and eternal kingdoms.

Lesson

IV. GOD'S PLAN (v. 10*b*)

"Thy will be done in earth, as it is in heaven."

Whenever we pray, it should be in accord with God's will. Ultimately we should say, "God, Your will be done." The literal Greek text would read something like this: "Whatever You wish to have happen, let it happen immediately." The Greek text also mentions heaven first, not earth. As God's will is done in heaven, let it be so on earth.

In Psalm 40:8 King David prays, "I delight to do thy will, O my God." He wanted to know and do God's will. Christ expresses the same desire in John 4:34 when He says, "My food is to do the will of him that sent me, and to finish his work." In John 6:38 He says, "I came down from heaven, not to do mine own will but the will of him that sent me." In Mark 3:35 Jesus says, "Whosoever shall do the will of God, the same is my brother, and my sister, and mother." When Christ was in the Garden of Gethsemane just before His crucifixion, He prayed to the Father, "Not my will, but thine, be done" (Luke 22:42). Jesus always prayed that God's will would be done.

What do we mean when we say "thy will be done"? People generally have either a negative or positive perspective when they pray that. First let's look at those who pray for God's will with a wrong understanding.

A. The Negative Perspective

    1. Examining the negative viewpoints

        a) Praying with bitter resentment

            Some people pray "thy will be done" with bitterness because they believe there is no escape from the inevitable. Such an attitude comes from an improper knowledge of God. These people think of God as oppressive, selfish, and cruel. Commentator William Barclay said, "A man may say, 'Thy will be done,' in a tone of defeated resignation. He may say it, not because he wishes to say it, but because he has accepted the fact that he cannot possibly say anything else; he may say it because he has accepted the fact that God is too strong for him, and that it is useless to batter his head against the walls of the universe" (*The Gospel of Matthew*, vol. 1 [Philadelphia: Westminster, 1975], p. 212).

Sometimes people become bitter when they lose a child, a spouse, or a limb. You may have experienced situations in your life that caused you to say "thy will be done" with clenched teeth. Eleventh-century Persian poet Omar Khayyam had that perspective of God. He said this in verse 69 of the *Rubaiyat*, a collection of his four-lined epigrams:

But helpless Pieces of the Game He plays
Upon this Checkerboard of Nights and Days;
   Hither and thither moves, and checks, and slays,
And one by one back in the Closet lays.

This Persian poet saw God as a checker player with total power over the playing pieces, moving them at His whims and putting them in the closet when He was done. In verse 70 he likened God to a polo player with a bat and man as a ball, which has absolutely no choice about where it goes:

   The Ball no question makes of Ayes and Noes,
   But Here or There as strikes the Player goes;
     And He that tossed you down into the Field,
   He knows about it all—He knows—HE knows!

b) Praying with passive resignation

(1) Explaining passive resignation

Some people pray, "Go ahead and do whatever You want to do, Lord. I can't do anything about it anyway." That kind of attitude doesn't come so much from an improper knowledge of God as it does from a lack of faith. A person who prays for God's will with bitter resentment doesn't see God as a loving, caring Father whose heart breaks over man's pain. He doesn't see the magnitude of God's love as expressed in Christ's death. The person who prays out of passive resignation lacks faith and thinks, "I shouldn't get too concerned about this matter because prayer doesn't do much anyway." He has an attitude of defeat.

I can personally identify with that attitude. After my freshman year in college, I was in a bad car accident. I was thrown out of a car going nearly seventy-five miles per hour and slid down the highway, losing some of my back side. I also had third- degree burns and other injuries. I was wide awake the whole time; I never lost consciousness. Fortunately I didn't break any bones. I walked off the highway and stood by the side. I can remember vividly among the many thoughts that passed through my mind, one was, "All right, God. If you're going to fight this way, I give up! I can't handle this!" I knew God had called me into the ministry, but I was starting to focus my life in another direction. I think God used that experience to get my attention.

At the time of the accident, I had an attitude of passive resignation. I thought, "Lord, if You're so concerned about me going into the ministry that You're going to let the car I was riding in turn over with five other kids in it and let me get injured, then I give up." I resigned myself to the fact that my other plans were over. But over the three months following that accident, my passive resignation turned into an active commitment. God began to refine my life and draw me to Himself.

There are people who pray "thy will be done" when they really have on their mind: "God, I don't think my prayer is going to do any good, so I'm just going to ask for Your will to be done because I know it will be anyway." Do you pray that way? Do you think the inevitable will happen and that your prayers don't make any difference? A person with such an attitude accepts God's will in a joyless, defeated way.

(2) Exemplifying passive resignation

I believe the primary reason many of us have a weak prayer life is because we don't believe our prayers will do anything anyway. We talk to the Lord about something and then forget about it, as if we already knew in advance that what we asked for probably wouldn't happen.

A classic illustration of that appears in Acts 12. Peter was in prison, and the church was concerned. But Peter had been in jail before (Acts 4:3); what was the church so concerned about? The reason the church was so upset about Peter's imprisonment was because James, the brother of John, had just been imprisoned and beheaded under Herod Antipas (Acts 12:1-2). The people in the church feared that Peter would be beheaded too. So they went to the house of Mary (the mother of John Mark) and prayed that the Lord would release Peter (v. 5). During their prayer meeting, an angel of the Lord freed Peter from his chains.

Peter went to Mary's house, where the prayer meeting was being held, and knocked on the door. A maid named Rhoda came to the door and heard Peter's voice and ran to tell the other people that Peter was there. Now that was a fast answer to prayer: The prayer meeting was still going on, and Peter was already at the door! When Rhoda told everyone Peter was there, they didn't believe her. But she persisted and said, "Peter is here!" Then they said, "Perhaps it's his angel" (v. 15). That was a silly statement. Peter would've needed his angel more at the prison, not at the prayer meeting. Finally when the door was opened and Peter came in, everyone was astonished. Why? Because they probably didn't think their prayers would do any good. How easy it is for us to fall into a passive resignation that makes our prayers meaningless!

Is God's Will Always Done on Earth?

The statement "thy will be done in earth" assumes that God's will is not always done here. When we say "hallowed be thy name" are there times and places that God's name is not hallowed? Yes. When we say "thy kingdom come" are there hearts that reject His reign? There are. The same is true with the phrase "thy will be done in earth, as it is in heaven." Not everything that happens in the world is God's will. Otherwise that petition is pointless.

If you go into the house of a family who has lost a child to a fatal disease or an automobile accident, you may hear someone say, "It was the Lord's will for that to happen." Or you may hear of a mother dying from cancer who is needed by her husband and children, and someone will say, "This is the Lord's will." Disasters such as floods, earthquakes, fires, train wrecks, airplane crashes, or famine are frequently explained away as being the Lord's will. But if you look at life with that kind of perspective, there will be no energy in your prayer life.

This may sound heretical, but God does not will for tragic things to happen. Jesus came into the world to stop the problems we have. Second Peter 3:9 tells us that God is "not willing that any should perish." There are people dying all over the world every day, but God does not will that they die without becoming saved and coming to a knowledge of the truth. Unfortunately, many people don't become saved before they die. So God's will is done in heaven, but it's not always done on earth.

(3) Eliminating passive resignation

You may say, "But God is sovereign. The only way tragic things can happen is if God allows them to happen." That's right, but that doesn't mean they are an expression of His will. It is not God's desire that people die and go to hell. Otherwise, why would He have come to destroy death and provide the salvation that keeps people from going to hell? Yet God allows man the choice to do good or evil. Although God is sovereign, He has allowed sin—He is allowing the cup of iniquity to become full before he pours out His wrath in the end times.

(a) Considering the framework of God's will

God is not responsible for sin or its consequences; He just tolerates it. It's difficult to understand how those two facts go together. In Matthew 10:28 Jesus says, "Fear not them who kill the body, but are not able to kill the soul; but rather fear him who is able to destroy both soul and body in hell." God can destroy both body and soul in hell. Satan is one of those who will be destroyed. Can we conclude that it must be the will of God for

81

Satan and unbelievers to be destroyed? No, because 2 Peter 3:9 says that He is "not willing that any should perish." God's holiness and justice must provide a way to deal with sin, even though it's not His desire to punish sinners.

In John 5:40, Jesus says to the Jewish religious leaders, "Ye will not come to me, that ye might have life." In Matthew 23:37, He weeps over the city of Jerusalem and says, "O Jerusalem, Jerusalem, thou that killest the prophets, and stonest them who are sent unto thee, how often would I have gathered thy children together, even as a hen gathereth her chickens under her wings, and ye would not!" Through the prophet Jeremiah, God said, "This evil people, who refuse to hear my words. . . . I will fill all the inhabitants of this land . . . with drunkenness. And I will dash them one against another, even the fathers and the sons together . . . I will not pity, nor spare, nor have mercy, but destroy them" (Jer. 13:10, 13-14). After He warned His people about the coming judgment, He said, "If ye will not hear it [i.e., obey what I say], my soul shall weep in secret places for your pride; and mine eye shall weep bitterly, and run down with tears" (v. 17). Why would God weep if the Israelites didn't obey Him? Because He didn't want to have to destroy them.

b) Considering the freedom of man's choice

John 3:16 says, "God so loved the world, that he gave his only begotten Son." Why did God give His Son? So men might be saved from judgment. Then why did God allow sin to come into the world? This illustration might help answer that question. I once told my oldest son Matt, "When you leave this house, you will be on your own." Now if my son should happen to go out and enter a life of sin, would that be my will? No. My heart would break if that happened. Yet he lives

82

within the framework of choice. Just because I give him freedom doesn't mean he will use that freedom the way I want him to. I may have to deal with the consequences of his sins and make him accountable for them.

God is a loving Father. In a general sense, every person—including a believer—can express his own will. He can choose to sin or be righteous. Yet God doesn't want anyone to choose sin. Some time ago a person with a Calvinistic perspective said to me, "God's will is expressed in your sin." I said I didn't see any biblical support for what he said. He responded, "But that's the only logical conclusion on why a sovereign God allows sin." I told him, "We can't explain the paradox. Our minds and God's mind don't work the same way." Habakkuk 1:13 says that God is "of purer eyes than to behold evil." James 1:13 says that God does not tempt any man to sin. Thus, God would never lead us to sin as an expression of His will. Yet He has given us the freedom to choose to sin.

Why Does God Allow Sin to Exist?

No one really knows why God allows sin, but let me give you one possible answer that theologians have discussed for a long time. Lucifer was one of God's angels, and he rebelled against God. We don't know how he fell; his pride couldn't have come from within him because he was perfect. Nor could it have come from the environment around him because it was perfect too. Only God knows how Lucifer sinned. When Lucifer fell, God had two options. One was to destroy him immediately. If He had done that, some of the angels might have thought, "There must be something about sin that upsets God. I wonder if He is afraid of it or its potential?" With that possibility, God could have been spending all eternity wiping out rebellious angels.

The other option was to let evil run its full course so that it would spend itself. God allowed evil to exist so that others could see that if it had a point to prove, it would be given time to do so. So the Lord probably chose that option rather than have the possibility of rebellion occurring again and again. He is letting Lucifer's rebellion go full circle until it runs itself out, just as a comet eventually fades out, never to rise again. That way, all eternity will be preserved from the recurrence of a sinful expression. God let fallen angels and all mankind follow after sin, but He has also provided mankind a way of escape from it. Right now in His wisdom, God is allowing evil to run its course because He knows the big picture of all eternity better than we do. Yet even though God lets it run its course, that doesn't mean He wants it to exist. He tolerates sin so that it may eventually be destroyed. Thus, we can't say "thy will be done" out of bitter resentment or passive resignation, thinking that we must accept tragedies as a part of God's will. They aren't His will.

c) Praying with theological reservation

The person with theological reservation says, "God will do what He wants to do, so there is no sense in me praying about it." There is no pleading or intensity in this person's prayers. Anyone who takes this approach to prayer will never have much of a prayer life. Don't say, "I don't need to pray because everything is cut and dried. God's will is already settled. God is up there, He is big, and He runs everything."

There is an interesting story the liberal Protestant theologian Reinhold Niebuhr loved to tell, which is documented in the book *Courage to Change*, by June Bingham (New York: Kelley, 1961).

One day, Niebuhr asked his daughter if she would like to go for a walk. She said no. He then told her that the fresh air and exercise would be good for her, so she went along. After the walk, he asked her, "Now didn't you enjoy that?" His daughter replied, "No; I didn't really want to go. I only went because you were bigger."

Many children probably do things only because adults are bigger than they are. Some people have the same view of God. They see Him as an overarching individual who gives them no choice. But when you view God that way, it's hard to have the joyful heart David had when he said to the Lord, "Oh, how I love thy law!" (Ps. 119:97). Praying to God with an attitude of theological reservation will make your prayers impersonal.

To pray with an attitude of bitter resentment, passive resignation, or theological reservation is fatalistic. When we pray "thy will be done" we're not looking at God as One who has an overarching will that our prayers can't change. Our prayers do have an effect.

84

2. Eradicating the negative viewpoints

   a) The parable of persistence

   There is an illustration in Luke 18 of what prayer can
   do. Jesus gave a parable to His disciples "to this end,
   that men ought always to pray, and not to faint" (v.
   1). You are to always pray. Don't ever quit or become
   weary.

   Verses 2-3 say, "There was in a city a judge, who
   feared not God, neither regarded man. And there
   was a widow in that city; and she came unto him,
   saying, Avenge me of mine adversary." The widow
   was basically telling the judge, "I've been wronged.
   Please take care of this injustice and make it right."
   Verses 4-5 continue, "[The judge] would not for a
   while; but afterward he said within himself, Though
   I fear not God, nor regard man, yet because this
   widow troubleth me, I will avenge her, lest by her
   continual coming she weary me." The judge got so
   sick of hearing from the woman that he did what she
   requested just to get rid of her. Children are like that
   with their parents. They'll ask if they can do something, and if you say no, sometimes they will persist
   until you say yes.

   What was the Lord teaching in that parable? Let's
   look at what He says in verses 6-8: "Hear what the
   unjust judge saith. And shall not God avenge his
   own elect, who cry day and night unto him, though
   he bear long with them? I tell you that he will avenge
   them speedily." If an unjust judge will give justice to
   a persistent woman, what will our just, loving, caring
   Father give to us? By the way, Jesus was not drawing
   a parallel between the judge and God; He was
   making a parallel between the widow and the peti-
   tioner.

   b) The principle of persistence

   There are two things we can learn from the widow in
   Luke 18. First, she refused to accept an unjust situation. Second, she persisted with her case. She did not
   tolerate the injustice done to her, and she persisted
   until things were made right. That tells us we have a
   right to refuse to accept certain situations in the
   world. We can refuse to accept the way things are

and pray persistently that God will do them the way they should be done.

When we pray "thy will be done" we're not just saying, "Whatever happens, I will accept it." In actuality, praying for God's will is nothing less than rebellion. When we pray for God's will to be done, we are praying against the fallen state of the world. We are rebelling against accepting as normal what is really abnormal. We are to pray against every plan, deed, word, and movement that is at odds with the will of God. Such a prayer appears in Revelation 6, where the souls of slain believers cry out to God, "How long, O Lord, holy and true, dost thou not judge and avenge our blood on them that dwell on the earth?" (v. 10). It was typical of David to pray in the psalms, "Lord, don't let Your enemies prosper don't let unrighteous men fare well."

To pray for God's will to be done on earth is to rebel against the evil of the world, the inevitability of sin and the consequences of sin. We are to bang on the gates of heaven with our prayers. Don't let bitter resentment, passive resignation, or theological reservation hold you back. Don't assume that everything that happens is God's will, because it's not. I can't say that the families I've seen break up were allowed to do so because it was God's will. If a church collapses or a believer sins, don't say it's God's will. We need to pray for God's will to be done on earth because it's not being done. Our prayers are not to be passive. That's why Jesus said to pray always and not lose heart (Luke 18:1).

How Long Should We Pray a Specific Petition?

Sometimes when we pray with persistence, things won't happen immediately the way we want them to. For example, Christians have been praying for Christ's return for a long time. In Revelation 22:20 John writes, "Even so, come, Lord Jesus." We say, "Lord, You don't deserve the treatment You are receiving on earth. Come set up Your kingdom and be glorified." Christians have prayed that for the last two thousand years, and we will keep on praying that. When we pray for Christ's return, we are rebelling against the fallen state of the world and the things that go against the Lord Jesus Christ and His precious Word. We ought to have the rebellious spirit in our prayers.

c) The practice of persistence

In the Garden of Gethsemane, Jesus prayed a prayer of rebellion. He says in Matthew 26:39, "O my Father, if it be possible, let this cup pass from me; nevertheless, not as I will, but as thou wilt." He didn't stop there. In verse 42 He says, "O my Father, if this cup may not pass away from me except I drink it, thy will be done." Then He prayed the same thing again a third time (v. 44). We also read that after each prayer, Christ went to His disciples and found them asleep.

Why did Christ say the same prayer three times? He never accepted the status quo. He didn't say to God, "I have to go to the cross; it's Your will." Instead, He said, "Father, does it have to be this way? I rebel against the power of sin to take My life. I rebel against the necessity of bearing sin and against the things that violate the sanctity of Your holy universe." In the midst of His rebellion against the fallen state of the world, the disciples were asleep. Why? Because they were indifferent.

What is your prayer life like? Are you praying "thy will be done in earth" because it isn't always being done? Are you persistent not for personal gain but for God's glorification?

Focusing on the Facts

1. Give some examples of answered prayer from Scripture (see p. 72).
2. What exhortations are we given in the Bible about the frequency of our prayers (see p. 73)?
3. What are some questions people have about the relationship between prayer and God's will (see p.73)?
4. The truths about the effectiveness of prayer and the sovereignty of God appear to be paradoxical to us. What do such paradoxes reveal about man in comparison to God (see p. 73)?
5. What are we to do when we come across paradoxes in Scripture (see p. 75)?
6. Prayer is to be said with _____ words centered on the _____ thoughts (see p. 75).
7. How does the literal Greek text of the phrase "thy will be done" read (see p. 77)?

8. What did Christ say about doing God's will (see p. 77)?
9. How do those who pray with bitter resentment view God and His will (see pp. 77-78)?
10. From what does the attitude of passive resignation in prayer come? In what way does a person with such an attitude accept God's will (see pp. 78-79)?
11. How do we know that the people at the prayer meeting in Acts 12 were praying out of passive resignation (see p. 80)?
12. What does the phrase "thy will be done" assume (see p. 80)?
13. How do people usually explain tragic events? Are they right? Explain, using Scripture to support your answer (see p. 81).
14. According to John 5:40, Matthew 23:37, and Jeremiah 13, what is God's will? In light of that answer, why do people sin (see pp. 82-83)?
15. Discuss why God may have allowed sin to exist (see pp. 83-84).
16. Describe the attitude of the person who prays with theological reservation (see p. 84).
17. What did Christ say about prayer in Luke 18:1 (see p. 85)?
18. What was Christ teaching in the parable in Luke 18 (see pp. 85-86)?
19. In what way are our prayers to be a form of rebellion (see p. 86)?

Pondering the Principles

1. James 5:16 says, "The prayer of a righteous man is powerful and effective" (NIV*). What kind of man prays effectively? Read Psalm 24:3-5 and 1 Timothy 2:8. According to those verses, how are we to come before the Lord? If we expect God to answer our prayers and be glorified through our prayers, then we must be committed to living a righteous life. What are some things you can do to continually ensure that your heart is pure when you come before God? When your life is right, you will sense true peace and joy as you come before the Lord in prayer.

2. Requests usually make up the majority of our prayers. A frequent complaint some people have about prayer is that they wonder why God hasn't given them what they asked for. According to Matthew 6:25-33, what should we be most concerned about? What does James 4:3 say is one reason that some prayer requests are not answered? With those things in mind, what type of prayer requests would be acceptable to God?

3. When we pray, it's important that our petitions be in line with God's will. Here is an activity that may give you insight into

*New International Version.

some new things you can be praying for: Write down some things you know that God would like to see happen on earth. (Try to get as many of your ideas as possible from the Bible.) Add to that list some things you know God would want to do through your life. From your list, you will get new ideas on how you can pray in harmony with God's will.

4. The paradox between God's sovereignty and effective prayer cannot be completely explained. We must trust what the Bible says about the effectiveness of prayer in the midst of God's plans. After having read about the negative perspectives of prayer, you now know what attitudes we should not have when we pray. Based on what you have learned, what kind of attitudes do you think would make up a healthy perspective toward prayer?

6
The Plan of Prayer—Part 2

Outline

Introduction
A. The Pharisaic Focus in Prayer
B. The Proper Focus in Prayer

Review
I. God's Paternity (v. 9a)
II. God's Priority (v. 9b)
III. God's Program (v. 10a)

Lesson
IV. God's Plan (v. 10b)
A. The Negative Perspective
  1. Examining the negative viewpoints
    a) Praying with bitter resentment
    b) Praying with passive resignation
    c) Praying with theological reservation
  2. Eliminating the negative viewpoints
    a) The parable of persistence
    b) The principle of persistence
    c) The practice of persistence
B. The Positive Perspective
  1. The specifics of praying for God's will
    a) God's comprehensive will
     (1) The definition
     (2) The Scripture
      (a) Jeremiah 51:29
      (b) Isaiah 14:24
      (c) Isaiah 14:26-27
      (d) Ephesians 1:9-11
     (3) The application
    b) God's compassionate will

      (1) The definition
      (2) The Scripture
         (*a*) Luke 13:34
         (*b*) John 5:40
         (*c*) Jeremiah 13:17
         (*d*) 2 Peter 3:9
         (*e*) 1 Timothy 2:4
   c) God's commanding will
      (1) The definition
      (2) The Scripture
         (*a*) Acts 5:29
         (*b*) Romans 6:16
         (*c*) Psalm 119
  2. The struggle in praying for God's will
    a) The request to be sacrificial
    b) The result of being sacrificial

Introduction

In Matthew 6:9-13 we read the Disciples' Prayer: "Our Father, who art in heaven, hallowed be thy name. Thy kingdom come. Thy will be done in earth, as it is in heaven. Give us this day our daily bread. And forgive us our debts, as we forgive our debtors. And lead us not into temptation, but deliver us from evil. For thine is the kingdom, and the power, and the glory, forever. Amen." Christ taught that prayer in response to the disciples' request in Luke 11:1, where they say "Lord, teach us to pray." It is the pattern for prayer; it is the framework that gives us insight into how we are to pray. When God told Moses to build a Tabernacle, He gave him a design to follow (Ex. 25-31). Jesus gave us a pattern for prayer in Matthew 6. Just as a blueprint is important for building a house, the pattern Christ gave us is important for our prayers. He wasn't giving us words to recite, although the words are true and lovely. He was giving us a structure on which to build our prayer life.

  A. The Pharisaic Focus in Prayer

    The main thrust of the Disciples' Prayer is that it focuses on God, not us. In Matthew chapters 5-7, Jesus confronts the false, man-centered religious system of the Pharisees and the Scribes. Their prayers, among other things, were inadequate. He deals with their prayers beginning in Matthew 6:5, attacking the self-centered focus they had. They prayed before other men to show how pious they were. The Pharisees and scribes didn't want anything to do with private prayer. They were involved in public prayer only so they could be on display. Their prayers focused on their own will and selfish desires. They engaged in vain repetitions in an attempt to badger God into giving them what they wanted, just as pagans tried to appease their deities. The Pharisees and scribes prayed as if they were saying, "God, You had better listen because I have some interesting information You need to know." They acted as if God were not omniscient. Their prayers were like those described in James 4:3: "Ye ask . . . that ye may consume it upon your lusts." Jesus said that their prayers needed to be God-centered.

B. The Proper Focus in Prayer

The proper way to pray is to begin by concentrating on God. The introduction, "Our Father, who art in heaven," calls for our attention to be on Him. It also affirms that God is a loving Father who can meet all the needs of His children because He has all the eternal resources of heaven at His disposal. When we pray, we are coming before a holy, almighty God who is also our loving Father. We can come to Him not in fear but joy. We can come before Him not wondering if He can provide what we need but knowing that He has the resources of eternity at His disposal.

When we introduce ourselves into God's presence, we are to focus on Him first. The first petitions in the Disciples' Prayer confirm that: "Hallowed be thy name. Thy kingdom come. Thy will be done in earth, as it is in heaven" (Matt. 6:9-10). Those petitions come before we say, "Give us. . . . Forgive us. . . . Lead us" (vv. 11-13). Prayer begins with acknowledging God, His holy name, His kingdom, and His will. So many of us rush into God's presence stating our petty desires and petitions without affirming who He is and establishing that His causes are in our hearts.

Every element of the Disciples' Prayer focuses on God. Even the petitions that relate to us—the petitions for our daily bread, forgiveness, and protection in the midst of temptation—really depend on God. It is He who must provide for, forgive, and lead us. "Our Father, who art in heaven" speaks of God's paternity. "Hallowed be thy name" refers to God's priority. "Thy kingdom come" speaks of God's program. "Thy will be done" is in regard to God's plan. "Give us this day our daily bread" is a request for God's provision. "Forgive us our debts, as we forgive our debtors" refers to God's pardon. "Lead us not into temptation, but deliver us from evil" points to God's protection. And the words, "For thine is the kingdom, and the power, and the glory, forever," speak to God's preeminence. Thus, prayer is primarily an act of worship. It is an action that helps sanctify you. don't pray to change God; pray to change yourself.

Review

I. GOD'S PATERNITY (v. 9a; see pp. 22-31)

II. GOD'S PRIORITY (v. 9b; see pp. 36-49)

III. GOD'S PROGRAM (v. 10a; see pp. 59-69)

Lesson

IV. GOD'S PLAN (v. 10b)

"Thy will be done in earth, as it is in heaven."

This is the third petition in the Disciples' Prayer. It is essential that in all our prayers, we ultimately seek for God's will to be done. We should never desire to usurp His will or change it so that it be conformed to our own will. Amy Carmichael, an early twentieth century missionary to India, wrote,

> And shall I pray to change Thy will my Father
> Until it be according to mine?
> But no, Lord, no, that shall never be
> Rather I pray Thee blend my human will with Thine.

Prayer is not for us to bend God to our will but to bend us to God's will.

What Can We Learn from the Angels?

God's will is already done in heaven, for the angels do His will. Let's look at how they accomplish that, because if we are going to know how to do God's will on earth, we will need to know how it's done in heaven.

1. Angels do God's will unwaveringly

   The angels don't discuss with God what they plan to do. They don't debate with Him. On earth, the Lord often needs to prod us before we get moving, but in heaven there is an unwavering commitment to do God's will.

2. Angels do God's will completely

   There are no alternatives to doing God's will. Everything is done as He desires. There are no omissions.

3. Angels do God's will sincerely

   The angels are eager to do God's will. They stand waiting for His commands so that they can hurry to accomplish whatever needs to be done.

4. Angels do God's will willingly

   How many wills are there in heaven? One. The Disciples' Prayer says, "Thy will be done in earth, as it is in heaven" (Matt. 6:10). God's will is done in heaven, since it is the only will existing. There were two wills at one time, but possessor of the second one (Satan) got kicked out. The angels follow God's desires willingly, because His is the only will there is.

5. Angels do God's will fervently

   The angels are very aggressive in doing God's will.

6. Angels do God's will readily (Matt. 26:53)

7. Angels do God's will swiftly (Dan. 9:20-21)

8. Angels do God's will constantly (Heb. 1:13-14)

   Psalm 103:20 sums up the angels' commitment to do God's will: "Bless the Lord, ye his angels . . . that do his commandments." The list above describes how God's will is done in heaven. Likewise, we should do His will on earth unwaveringly, completely, sincerely, willingly, fervently, readily, swiftly, and constantly.

You may say, "Now that I know how we should do God's will, I'm committed to doing it in those ways. But what exactly does it mean to do His will?" Basically, it involves making God's causes your primary concerns. This statement should help conceptualize what we are talking about: The death of self is the beginning of a true prayer life. Only when self dies does true prayer begin. When you are more concerned about yourself and your causes, you'll become the primary focus in your prayers. But true prayer is dominated by God's name, kingdom, and will—not ours. That's the mind-set David had when he prayed, "I delight to do thy will, O my God" (Ps. 40:8). Jesus had the same thing in mind when He said, "My food is to do the will of him that sent me" (John 4:34). God's name is to be hallowed, His kingdom is to rule, and His will is to be done on earth as it is in heaven.

A. The Negative Perspective (see pp. 77-87)

   1. Examining the negative viewpoints (see pp. 77-84)

      a) Praying with bitter resentment (see pp. 77-78)

To pray "thy will be done" does not mean you say, "God, let Your will be done. You're too big anyway; I can't fight your plans." Some people view God as a cosmic killjoy who spoils everyone's fun and rains on their parades. Don't view God's will as an inevitable fate.

      b) Praying with passive resignation (see pp. 78-84)

A person who prays with passive resignation has an indifferent attitude, saying, "Whatever happens, will happen." There is a song called "Que Sera Sera" that has the line, "Whatever will be, will be." Bitter resentment is based on a lack of knowledge about God, and passive resignation is built on a lack of faith. Such a person doesn't really believe God will change things to do what you ask Him when it's in accord with His will.

      c) Praying with theological reservation (see p. 84)

Some people pray "thy will be done" and think of their prayers as having little or no impact on God's plans. They allow their perspective on God's sovereignty to eliminate their persistence in prayer. A man once said to me, "I believe that even your sin is God's will. He is involved in causing you to sin. After all, He's sovereign." That man had a warped view of God's sovereignty, and such a view will destroy the life in your prayers. If your theology on God's will has brought you to a point of indifference in your prayers, then your theology isn't biblical.

   2. Eradicating the negative viewpoints (see pp. 85-87)

      a) The parable of persistence (see p. 85)

      b) The principle of persistence (see pp. 85-86)

God is sovereign, and how your prayer life fits into His plans is a very difficult mystery that can't be explained. Instead, we need to concern ourselves with obedience and persistence. In Matthew 26 our

Lord prays the same prayer three times in the Garden of Gethsemane. He also gives an illustration of praying with persistence in Luke 18. So don't say "thy will be done" with bitter resentment, passive resignation, or theological reservation.

The prayer "thy will be done" is to be said with an attitude of rebellion. We aren't merely giving in to God when we pray that prayer. Jesus says in Luke 18:1 that we are to pray always without losing heart. We are to rebel against the world's fallen state. Our prayers should be like this: "God, your will is not being done in this world. Satan has too much power here. Your will is not being done in the hearts of men, in my life, and in the lives of disobedient believers." When we pray for God's will to be done, we are rebelling against the rejection of Christ and the disobedience of believers.

Theologian David Wells said, "To come to an acceptance of life 'as it is,' to accept it on its own terms—which means acknowledging the inevitability of the way it works—is to surrender a Christian view of God" ("Prayer: Rebelling Against the Status Quo," *Christianity Today* [2 November 1979], p. 33). God doesn't accept the way the world is, or He wouldn't be busy changing it. He wouldn't have come into the world to destroy the one who has the power of death. He wouldn't have promised a millennial rule where there will be no diseases or tears. Likewise, we should not accept things the way they are. To pray for God's will is to rebel against the world and everything that is a result of sin. Even though God has permitted sin to run its course in human history, it's not the expression of His loving will for man.

c)   The practice of persistence (see p. 87)

Christ is the classic illustration of rebelling against the world. In John 2 when He saw the merchants and moneychangers in the Temple, He didn't say, "That's God's will." He rebelled. He was indignant with righteous wrath. He made a whip and started lashing at people and turning over tables. And He didn't do that once; He did it twice! The second time He was so furious that everyone left without taking even a penny with them (Mark 11:15-16). The people were in the Temple to make money; imagine how angry Jesus must have been to make them leave without their money. Why did Christ react that way? He wouldn't accept the status quo. He didn't tolerate the way the world is with its sorrow, sin, and sickness. That's why He healed people. He raised the dead to stop people's tears as well as bring Himself glory. Christ's death on the cross rebelled against the status quo. He didn't accept the way the world was, and neither should we.

Our prayer should be, "Thy will be done on earth, as it is in heaven." One thing that amazes me is that Christ prayed persistently for God's will, even though He already knew everything that would happen. He fought the manifestation of sin and sought God's will. He must have known that His nightly prayers to the Father in the Garden would do some good. He knew prayer was effective. One reason we don't rebel against the status quo in our society is that things have been comfortable for us in the world. Now things are becoming less comfortable for those of us who live in America, but I think that's great because it will have a trememdous effect on the way the church prays.

Why Do People Pray So Little for the Church?

Sometimes I feel like we don't pray enough for our churches. Some people might say, "We need to have a prayer seminar" or, "We need to teach what the Bible says about prayer." To do those things might help, but they aren't the best solutions. Does the reason we don't pray enough have to do with our weak wills? A lack of commitment? I don't think so because it's possible to make people excited about almost anything. I think the reason we don't pray enough is that we don't believe our prayers will make a difference. Why do we think that? Because we perceive prayer as a way to change our circumstances when we should view it as a way to change ourselves. Prayer is not for the purpose of changing our circumstances so much as it is to change how we relate to them.

When we come into God's presence in worship and say, "hallowed be thy name," "thy kingdom come," "thy will be done," we are brought into conformity with His person. When that happens, our circumstances will become different because we will be bringing different attitudes to them. Even beyond that, I do believe that God changes circumstances. I've prayed for people to become saved and have had some of

98

those prayers answered. Not only does God sovereignly choose who becomes saved, but He also chooses the methods that will be used to lead the person to salvation. Sometimes we are part of His methods.

James 5:16 says, "The effectual, fervent prayer of a righteous man availeth much." Lack of persistence in prayer will lead you to strike a truce with things that are wrong. We have lost our anger and passion. We don't storm the throne of God, as early twentieth-century evangelist William Biederwolf used to say. God loves heroic faith. We don't storm the gates of heaven enough. Our prayers are to rebel against the world.

B. The Positive Perspective

What are we really praying for when we say "thy will be done"? There are three terms that can be used to help describe God's will in an understandable way. To just use the words *God's will* is too general.

1. The specifics of praying for God's will

    a) God's comprehensive will

        (1) The definition

            This refers to God's vast, all-inclusive will. This aspect of His will completely embodies the earth, heaven, and hell. It encompasses the allowance of sin and letting it run its course. The consummation of the ages; the establishment of the kingdom; the eternal state; and everything in heaven, hell, and any other place is within God's comprehensive will.

        (2) The Scripture

            (a) Jeremiah 51:29—In reference to Babylon, this verse says, "Every purpose of the Lord shall be performed." There is no question that God's plan is always being carried out. The plan of the ages is on track. God always works out His ultimate purposes.

            (b) Isaiah 14:24—"The Lord of hosts hath sworn, saying, Surely as I have thought, so shall it come to pass; and as I have purposed, so shall it stand." When God has a thought, it will become a reality. Whatever God purposes will come to pass.

99

(c) Isaiah 14:26-27—"This is the purpose that is purposed upon the whole earth, and this is the hand that is stretched out upon the nations. for the Lord of hosts hath purposed, and who shall annul it?"

God has purposes that will come to pass. For example, it is not God's desire for people to be ill, but it is within His purpose to allow illness to accomplish His own ends. It isn't His desire that people die, but it is within His comprehensive purpose to use death for His glory. We know that "all things work together for good to them that love God, to them who are the called according to his purpose" (Rom. 8:28). Although God does not will evil, He takes the things that happen in our lives and puts them together for good.

(d) Ephesians 1:9-11—God has "made known unto us the mystery of his will, according to his good pleasure which he hath purposed in himself" (v. 9). This verse tells us about salvation and forgiveness, which are parts of God's great encompassing purpose. Paul then talks about Jew and Gentile becoming one: "In the dispensation of the fullness of times he [will] gather together in one all things in Christ, both which are in heaven, and which are on earth . . . in whom also we have obtained an inheritance, being predestinated according to the purpose of him who worketh all things after the counsel of his own will" (vv. 10-11). God's great purpose—His eternal plan—is for a redeemed people, a unified church, and for a body of saints in eternity.

(3) The application

How do we pray for God's comprehensive will? In Revelation 22 verses 7 and 12, Jesus says, "Behold, I come quickly." John quoted those words in verse 20. That's the consummation of God's eternal plan. Do you know what John's response was? He said, "Even so, come, Lord Jesus" (Rev. 22:20).

How do we pray in accord with God's comprehensive will? By joyously awaiting the accomplishment of His divine ends. For example, you could say, "Lord, I know that someday You will call Your church from the world and have us be with Christ. May it be." Even though we know that's going to happen just as God has planned for it to, we are to pray in anticipation of that great hour. Do you ever get tired of your sinfulness, your physical body, and the anxieties of this world? I do. Sometimes in my prayers I will say, "Lord, I know what You plan to do someday, but go ahead and do it. The sooner the better!" That's praying according to God's comprehensive will.

b) God's compassionate will

    (1) The definition

        This aspect of God's will refers to His heart's desire. It's one part of His comprehensive will. You can see that kind of pattern in your life too. You have an overall plan for your life and career, and within that plan are personal desires. Not everything in your life is a personal desire, but usually you'll fit your desires into your life and career plans.

        There are some things God desires to happen that won't happen. In a sense, then, this aspect of God's will is unfulfilled. God has certain desires that men reject.

    (2) The Scripture

        (a) Luke 13:34—Jesus desired that Jerusalem be saved. He said, "O Jerusalem, Jerusalem, which killest the prophets, and stonest them that are sent unto thee, how often would I have gathered thy children together . . . and ye would not!"

        (b) John 5:40—Jesus said, "Ye will not come to me, that ye might have life."

        (c) Jeremiah 13:17—Jesus wasn't the only one who wept over lost men; the Father did too. When he warned Israel of coming judgment, He said, "My soul shall weep in secret places

for your pride; and mine eye shall weep bitterly, and run down with tears."

(d) 2 Peter 3:9—"The Lord . . . is longsuffering toward us, not willing that any should perish, but that all should come to repentance."

(e) 1 Timothy 2:4—God, our Savior, wills for "all to be saved, and to come unto the knowledge of the truth."

God's desire is for people to become saved, yet there will be many who will say, "Lord, Lord," to whom Christ will tell them, "I never knew you; depart from me" (Matt. 7:23). It's a mystery that God can be absolutely sovereign, yet man possess volition. We know that God earnestly desires for people to be saved. He even weeps over people who will never be redeemed. His tears show His desire.

c) God's commanding will

(1) The definition

This aspect of God's will is related to Christians. God's comprehensive will encompasses the universe, and in it, He is able to take suffering, sorrow, and sickness and make them work out for His eternal purposes. His compassionate will is confined to unbelievers, for God desires that the gospel be taken to the world. And God's commanding will is for Christians, since unbelievers don't have the capacity to do His will.

It is the ardent desire of God's heart that we who are His children obey Him completely and immediately with a willing heart. So when you say "thy will be done," you are praying for three things: The consummation of the world and the use of sin's consequences for God's eternal plan, the salvation of people who don't know God, and the obedience of every believer to God's commands.

How Do God's Will and Christ's Coming Kingdom Work Together?

When we studied the phrase "thy kingdom come" earlier in the Disciples' Prayer, we learned that there were three ways to bring the kingdom to earth. One way is through the conversion of unbelievers. Christ's kingdom comes when He establishes His reign in a person's heart. The second way His kingdom comes is by commitment. When a believer lives according to righteousness, peace, and joy in the Holy Spirit, the kingdom comes into his life. Third, Christ's kingdom will come at His second coming. He will establish an earthly rule.

There is a parallel between those three elements of the coming of Christ and the three elements of God's will being done. God's comprehensive will embraces the ultimate end of man's dominion on earth and the return of Christ to set up an eternal kingdom. His compassionate will embraces the conversion of unbelievers. And His commanding will is that there be commitment in our lives.

    (2) The Scripture

        (a) Acts 5:29 Peter said, "We ought to obey God rather than men."

        (b) Romans 6:16—Here, Paul essentially said, "If you have yielded yourselves as servants to God, why don't you obey Him?"

        (c) Psalm 119—David spoke of obedience in this magnificent psalm. Verse 27 says, "Make me to understand the way of thy precepts." In verses 30, 32-33 he says, "I have chosen the way of truth; thine ordinances have I laid before me. . . . I will run the way of thy commandments. . . . Teach me, O Lord, the way of thy statutes, and I shall keep it unto the end." Verse 47 reads, "I will delight myself in thy commandments." In verse 54 he says, "Thy statutes have been my songs." Verse 93 says, "I will never forget thy precepts; for with them thou hast given me life." And verse 97 reads, "Oh, how love I thy law!" David had a heart of obedience.

2. The struggle in praying for God's will

It's hard to pray "thy will be done." It's hard to be preoccupied with God in your prayers. Why is that? Because the major sin of the human heart is pride. You ask, "How can I get pride out of the way?" Paul gives us the answer in Romans 12:1: "I beseech you therefore, brethren, by the mercies of God, that ye present your bodies a living sacrifice, holy, acceptable unto God, which is your reasonable service. And be not conformed to this world, but be ye transformed by the renewing of your mind, that ye may prove what is that good, and acceptable, and perfect, will of God."

a) The request to be sacrificial

Until you lay your life on the altar as a living sacrifice—until your will is dead—God's will can't be manifest in your life. You say, "What then exactly is a living sacrifice?" Abraham is a good example of one. At God's request he took his son Isaac, gave him some wood to carry on his back, and went to Mount Moriah to offer him as a sacrifice (Gen. 22:1-3). During the trip he was probably thinking, "This is strange, God. You want me to slay my son on an altar, yet he is supposed to be the fulfillment of Your covenant promising me many descendents. That doesn't make sense." But Abraham went up Mount Moriah, strapped Isaac to the altar, and almost plunged a knife into his heart before the Lord stopped him (Gen. 22:9-12). If Abraham had killed his son, Isaac would have been a dead sacrifice, but Abraham would have been a living one. Why? Because he would have crucified all his dreams, goals, and desires. He literally would have died to himself in obedience to God. So the question isn't, Can you die for Christ? but, Can you live unselfishly for Christ? Our will is what stands in the way of praying for God's will to be done.

b) The result of being sacrificial

When you learn to pray in conformity with God's will, you will see a dramatic change in your life. Prayer is a sanctifying grace; it changes us. We can't use prayer to get God to satisfy our selfish desires. We shouldn't pray with incantations and vain repetition just to put on a show. When we come into God's presence, we want to hallow His name, bring His kingdom, and fulfill His will. In doing so, we enter into conformity with His blessed person.

Prayer is a means of progressive sanctification. John Hannah, associate professor of historical theology at Dallas Theological Seminary, said, "The end of prayer is not so much tangible answers as a deepening life of dependency" ("Prayer and the Sovereignty of God,"

Bibliotheca Sacra [October-December 1979], p. 353). Isn't that great? God will answer our prayers, but dependency on Him is the issue. Hannah further stated, "The call to prayer is a call primarily to love, submission, and obedience . . . the avenue of sweet, intimate, and intense fellowship of the soul with the infinite Creator" (p. 353). Thus we are to pray, "Thy will be done in earth, as it is in heaven."

Are You Allowing God to Make You a Useful Vessel?

W. Phillip Keller visited in Pakistan and tells of an interesting experience he had while there. After he read Jeremiah 18:2, which says, "Arise, and go down to the potter's house, and there I will cause thee to hear my words," he asked a skilled, elderly potter to show him how a masterpiece was created. In his book, *A Layman Looks at the Lord's Prayer* ([Chicago: Moody, 1976, 1985], pp. 92-97), this is what he wrote:

"In sincerity and earnestness I asked the old master craftsman to show me every step in the creation of a masterpiece. . . . On his shelves stood gleaming goblets, lovely vases, and exquisite bowls of breathtaking beauty.

"Then, crooking a bony finger toward me, he led the way to a small, dark, closed shed at the back of his shop. When he opened its rickety door, a repulsive, overpowering stench of decaying matter engulfed me. For a moment I stepped back from the edge of the gaping dark pit in the floor of the shed. 'This is where the work begins!' he said, kneeling down beside the black, nauseating hole. With his long, thin arm, he reached down into the darkness. His slim, skilled fingers felt around amid the lumpy clay, searching for a fragment of material exactly suited to his task.

"'I add special kinds of grass to the mud,' he remarked. 'As it rots and decays, its organic content increases the colloidal quality of the clay. Then it sticks together better.' Finally his knowing hands brought up a lump of dark mud from the horrible pit where the clay had been tramped and mixed for hours by his hard, bony feet.

"With tremendous impact the first verses from Psalm 40 came to my heart. In a new and suddenly illuminating way I saw what the psalmist meant when he wrote long ago, 'I waited patiently for the Lord, and he inclined unto me, and heard my cry. He brought me up also out of an horrible pit, out of the miry clay.' As carefully as the potter selected his clay, so

God used special care in choosing me. . . . The great slab of granite, carved from the rough rock of the high Hindu Kush mountains behind his home, whirled quietly. It was operated by a very crude, treadle-like device that was moved by his feet, very much like our antique sewing machines.

"As the stone gathered momentum, I was taken in memory to Jeremiah 18:3. 'Then I went down to the potter's house, and, behold, he wrought a work on the wheels.'

"But what stood out most before my mind at this point was the fact that beside the potter's stool, on either side of him, stood two basins of water. Not once did he touch the clay, now spinning swiftly at the center of the wheel, without first dipping his hands in the water. As he began to apply his delicate fingers and smooth palms to the mound of mud, it was always through the medium of the moisture of his hands. And it was fascinating to see how swiftly but surely the clay responded to the pressure applied to it through those moistened hands. Silently, smoothly, the form of a graceful goblet began to take shape beneath those hands. The water was the medium through which the master craftsman's will and wishes were being transmitted to the clay. His will actually was being done in earth.

"For me this was a most moving demonstration of the simple, yet mysterious truth that my Father's will and wishes are expressed and transmitted to me through the water of His own Word. . . .

"Suddenly, as I watched, to my utter astonishment, I saw the stone stop. Why? I looked closely. The potter removed a small particle of grit from the goblet. . . .Then just as suddenly the stone stopped again. He removed another hard object. . . .

"Suddenly he stopped the stone again. He pointed disconsolately to a deep, ragged gouge that cut and scarred the goblet's side. It was ruined beyond repair! In dismay he crushed it down beneath his hands. . . .

"'And the vessel that he made of clay was marred in the hand of the potter' (Jer. 18:4). Seldom had any lesson come home to me with such tremendous clarity and force. Why was this rare and beautiful masterpiece ruined in the master's hands? Because he had run into resistance. It was like a thunderclap of truth bursting about me!

"Why is my Father's will—His intention to turn out truly

beautiful people—brought to nought again and again? Why, despite His best efforts and endless patience with human beings, do they end up a disaster? Simply because they resist His will. . . .

"The sobering, searching, searing question I had to ask myself in the humble surroundings of that simple potter's shed was this: Am I going to be a piece of fine china or just a finger bowl? Is my life going to be a gorgeous goblet fit to hold the fine wine of God's very life from which others can drink and be refreshed? Or am I going to be just a crude finger bowl in which passersby will dabble their fingers briefly then pass on and forget all about it? It was one of the most solemn moments in all of my spiritual experiences.

"'Father, thy will be done in earth [in clay], in me, as it is done in heaven.'"

What about you? Are you becoming a goblet or a finger bowl? Keller later talked about the potter using a fine thread to cut his work from the wheel. That reminded him of being separated to do good works. Then the potter took the vessel and put it in an oven—which to Keller symbolized going through hardship—and his work was finally finished.

God wants to do His will in you. He wants to make you into a beautiful goblet. But if you resist, you will be made into a finger bowl. Instead of being used for the fine wine of God's great purposes, you'll be a bowl passersby dabble their fingers in. Are you willing to let God do His will in the clay of earth, as it is done in heaven? That should be the heart of your prayers.

Focusing on the Facts

1. Describe the way the Pharisees and scribes usually prayed. How does that compare with the way we should pray (see pp. 92-93)?
2. Explain how each part of the Lord's prayer focuses on God (see pp. 93-94).
3. Describe how God's will is done in heaven (see pp. 94-95).
4. What does it mean to do God's will (see p. 95)?
5. Instead of trying to understand how our prayers work in conjunction with God's will, what should we concern ourselves with (see p. 96)?
6. Give an example that shows Christ refused to accept the way things are in the world (see pp. 97-98).
7. What is probably the reason many Christians don't pray enough for the church? Why (see p. 98)?

8. What happens to our circumstances when we pray in conformity to God's person (see p. 98)?
9. What will a lack of persistence in prayer lead to (see p. 99)?
10. What does God's comprehensive will encompass? Cite Scripture that discuss God's comprehensive will (see pp. 99-100)?
11. How can we pray in harmony with God's comprehensive will (see p. 101)?
12. What is God's compassionate will? Use Scripture to support your answer. Will that aspect of God's will always be fulfilled? Explain (see pp. 101-2).
13. To whom is God's commanding will directed? How does God want those individuals to fulfill that aspect of His will (see p. 102)?
14. What did Peter, Paul, and David say about God's commanding will (see p. 103)?
15. Why is it hard for us to pray for God's will? How can we get over that problem (see pp. 103-4)?
16. Why would Abraham have been a living sacrifice if he had killed his son Isaac (see p. 104)?
17. What happens when you learn to pray in conformity with God's will? Explain (see p. 104).
18. Why is God sometimes unable to make a person all that He wants him to be (see pp. 106-7)?

Pondering the Principles

1. To do God's will is to be preoccupied with the same concerns that He is. In what ways are you fulfilling God's will in your life? Write down your answers. Now, reread the shaded box on pages 94-95. Do these characteristics mark the ways you are attempting to do God's will? What characteristics are you strong in? What characteristics do you need to work on? How would you benefit from working on those characteristics?

2. Are you allowing God to bring your life into conformity with His will? Consider the following when you answer that question: God expresses His will to us in the Bible. By reading it, we learn what God wants to see happen in our lives and on the earth. Do you set aside a time during your study of God's Word to think about ways to personally apply what you've learned? Are you faithful to immediately and persistently act upon the Bible truths you learn at church or in your Bible study? When we yield our lives completely to God, He can make us into masterpieces that fulfill His purposes on earth.

7
The Provision of Prayer—Part 1

Outline

Introduction
A. The Petition
    1. Explaining the complacency
    2. Examining the context
        a) The classifications of the petitions
            (1) The proper perspective
            (2) The perverted perspective
        b) The comprehensiveness of the petitions
B. The Problem

Review
  I. God's Paternity (v. 9*a*)
 II. God's Priority (v. 9*b*)
III. God's Program (v. 10*a*)
IV. God's Plan (v. 10*b*)

Lesson
V. God's Provision (v. 11)
    A. The Substance
        1. The extent of the petition
        2. The exercise of the petition
    B. The Source
        1. The sovereign provider
        2. The specific provisions
            a) God provides food for us
                (1) The variety of foods
                    (*a*) Plant foods
                        i) Grains
                        ii) Nuts
                        iii) Vegetables
                        iv) Fruits

     (*b*) Animal foods
      i) Meat
      ii) Dairy products
     (*c*) Condiments
    (2) The vast amount of foods
  b) God provides clothing for us
  c) God provides food for the plants and animals

Introduction

In this lesson of our study on the Disciples' Prayer, we are going to look at a familiar petition: "Give us this day our daily bread" (Matt. 6:11). The word *bread* opens up to us the simplicity of that petition, yet suggests a profound meaning that demands our careful study.

 Every time I read over the Disciples' Prayer, I am overwhelmed at the depth of it. Before I prepared this series I had never perceived the richness of the Lord's words in this prayer. There is almost a resistance in my heart to preach about it because it is such a masterpiece. I fear that would be like taking my own brush and touching up a Rembrandt or taking a chisel and trying to improve a sculpture done by Michelangelo. To do such would be out of my league, and I feel somewhat the same way when I approach the Lord's Prayer. I almost feel as if I should just read it and let it speak in its own majestic simplicity. So this study is simply an attempt to expound on the fullness of the Disciples' Prayer.

 A. The Petition

  In Matthew 6:11, we come to what seems to be the simplest petition of all: "Give us this day our daily bread." If we think there isn't much to say about that verse, we don't really understand all it's saying. So let's learn what we can.

  1. Explaining the complacency

   The petition "give us this day our daily bread" may seem somewhat irrelevant to us. When was the last time you prayed, "Lord, I plead with You to provide a meal for me"? I daresay most of us would sound more like this: "Lord, keep me from eating another meal. Teach me self-discipline because I need to lose weight." We usually have more than enough food for ourselves, so a request for food seems remote to us. When was the last time you were really desperate about getting food? It would seem more appropriate to preach on Matthew 6:11 in Bangladesh, Cambodia, or the Sahara Desert—not in America. But that only illustrates our lack of understanding about the marvelous truth contained in Matthew 6:11.

Do you know how much food there is in America? It's almost impossible to conceive of the amount of grain we can produce because of our technology, rich soil, and sophisticated machinery. There are new kinds of corn being tested in Mexico that would regenerate like grass does—you wouldn't have to reseed any land. Geneticists are now working on corn that will return nitrogen to the soil and save us about 13 million tons of fertilizer made by natural gas. That will save energy. One of the huge $100,000 combines that appear on farms today can harvest $118,000 worth of soybeans in a day. The harvests are unusually large because of near-perfect weather, good land, and improved technology. America's corn alone would fill 2 million jumbo hopper-cars, which would make a train long enough to stretch back and forth across the United States thirteen times. There are enough combines now that if they were put wheel-to-wheel, the entire state of Iowa could be harvested in one day. To do that with humans and farm animals would take 31 million people using 61 million horses and mules. Technology has given the United States incredible productivity. (These data appeared in a December 1980 *Time* magazine article.)

To us, saying "give us this day our daily bread" doesn't seem necessary. You can get any kind of bread you want. The petition for bread doesn't seem to be a major prayer request for Americans. What, then, is the application of that petition? Or should we just say, "Try to imagine you don't have any bread and that you are desperate enough for it that you pray for some." But that's an unreal situation. What application does Matthew 6:11 have for those who are well off?

2. Examining the context

Before we answer that question, let's remember the context of the passage. The Lord talks about prayer in Matthew 6:9-13 because that is one element of His kingdom. All twenty-eight chapters of Matthew's gospel present Christ as King, and chapters 5-7 present the principles of His kingdom, including the proper pattern for prayer. In the Disciples' Prayer are all the necessary ingredients for praying according to Christ's standard. One element is praying for our daily bread. That doesn't assume that we have or don't have our daily bread; Christ taught that it's one of the necessary parts of proper prayer. Because the Disciples' Prayer is a pattern for prayer, I make an effort to follow it, whether I'm praying with our church elders, at home, at my office, in my car, by myself, or in a group where two or three are gathered. I try to touch base with each of the principles Christ gave so that each prayer I utter would reflect the character of the Lord's prayer. I hope that's happening in your prayer life as well.

a)   The classifications of the petitions

There are basically two sections in the Disciples' Prayer. The first one deals with God and the second with man. God's glory is discussed first, and then man's need. The petitions "hallowed be thy name," "thy kingdom come," and "thy will be done" (Matt. 6:9-10) focus on God and His glory. "Give us this day our daily bread," "forgive us our debts," and "lead us not into temptation, but deliver us from evil" (Matt. 6:11-13) focus on man and his need. So God is the supreme issue in the prayer. Not until we put Him in His rightful place can we pray properly about our needs. We must first recognize God's name, kingdom, and will before we talk about man's need.

(1)   The proper perspective

Although the second section of the prayer deals with man's need, it doesn't set God aside. Just as in the first section of the prayer, God is exalted here. The fact that God gives us our daily bread, forgives our debts, and keeps us from temptation is an expression of His power and grace. So God's name is hallowed, His kingdom comes, and His will is done on earth when He takes care of us. The second half of the prayer brings God into human life. And we're not using the first three petitions to butter up God before we ask for what we want for our own sake. We are saying, "God, glorify Yourself in providing our daily needs, constantly forgiving us and leading us by Your Spirit. Be on display in Your world so that Your kingdom may come to earth." The petitions that mention our needs don't set God aside in any sense.

(2) The perverted perspective

My heart continually grieves over the current movement in Christianity that says we can demand things from God. A woman sent me a booklet and wrote, "I don't think you understand the true resource we have in prayer. You should read this booklet." The booklet repeatedly stated that we have a right to demand things from God because of who we are. But that isn't the point of prayer at all. We are to give God the privilege of revealing His glory by meeting our deepest human needs. We want God to be on display by His provision. If prayer becomes self-centered and selfish in any sense, it ceases to be the kind of prayer that is characteristic of our Lord's kingdom. Yet many people approach God to get something rather than to allow Him to glorify His name. We plead with God for what we want, and when we don't get it, we begin to question Him. Instead, we should allow God the right to choose how He wants to reveal His glory and majesty. Self-centered prayers won't be answered, and they tend to lead you to question God. That is a serious sin.

We are pragmatists in our society: We put a quarter into a machine to get a product, and we tend to approach prayer the same way. In fact, we do many things with the expectation of getting something back. Some people give in order to receive. They will hear a sermon on Luke 6:38, which says, "Give, and it shall be given unto you; good measure, pressed down, and shaken together, and running over," and give in hopes of getting even more back. The Lord will do that, but that's not to be our reason for giving. We are to give so that He can be glorified in how He responds to our gift, not for what we can get. One writer said, "If all the testimonies uttered during annual stewardship drives were to be believed, tithing could be commended for its profit and taught as an investment principle in Business Administration courses." Unfortunately, many of us use prayer as a way to get things rather than as an avenue for God to receive glory.

John 14:13 says the purpose of prayer is to bring glory to God.

b) The comprehensiveness of the petitions

Let's look at the three petitions that give God an opportunity to glorify Himself. "Give us this day our daily bread" (Matt. 6:11) speaks of our physical life. "Forgive us our debts, as we forgive our debtors" (Matt. 6:12) speaks of our mental life, and "lead us not into temptation, but deliver us from evil" (Matt. 6:13) refers to our spiritual life. Bread is our physical sustenance, forgiveness frees us from the anxiety and pain of guilt, and being led from temptation gives us spiritual direction. Bread takes care of the present, forgiveness takes care of the past, and spiritual help takes care of the future. All the dimensions and needs of life are covered in the Disciples' Prayer. It's amazing how God's infinite mind can reduce all there is of human need to three simple, profound statements.

B. The Problem

Everything ultimately is for the glory of God—and that includes prayer. Whatever we pray for, it's not for our gain but for God's glory. Prayer is not used to badger God and make Him change His mind. David C. Myers, in his book *The Human Puzzle* (New York: Harper and Row, 1978) says "Some petitionary prayers seem not only to lack faith in the inherent goodness of God but also to elevate humankind to a position of control over God. God, the Scriptures remind us, is omniscient and omnipotent, the sovereign ruler of the universe. For Christians to pray as if God were a puppet whose strings they yank with their prayers seems not only potentially superstitious but blasphemous as well.

"When prayer is sold as a device for eliciting health, success, and other favors from a celestial vending machine, we may wonder what is really being merchandised. Is this faith or is it faith's counterfeit, a glib caricature of true Christianity?"

Elton Trueblood said this: "In some congregations the Gospel has been diminished to the mere art of self-fulfillment. . . . Egocentricity is all that is left." There is much of that today in Christianity. Prayer for many is simply an egocentrical, self-indulgent exercise of demanding things from God. That's not right. The three petitions in Matthew 6:11-13, though directed at our essential needs, are ways that God's glory is revealed on earth. J. I. Packer said, "The prayer of a Christian is not an attempt to force God's hand, but a humble acknowledgment of helplessness and dependence."

Review

I. GOD'S PATERNITY (v. 9*a*; see pp. 22-31)

II. GOD'S PRIORITY (v. 9*b*; see pp. 36-49)

III. GOD'S PROGRAM (v. 10*a*; see pp. 59-69)

IV. GOD'S PLAN (v. 10*b*; see pp. 77-87, 94-107)

Lesson

Bread is a basic need of man. The word *bread* in Matthew 6:11 encompasses every physical need of man, and the petition is a prayer for our physical needs to be fulfilled. That's obvious in reading the verse, but in Western society, that petition is remote because we have so much. There are five points I'd like us to look at in relation to our physical needs: the substance, the source, the supplication, the seekers, and the schedule.

V. GOD'S PROVISION (v. 11)

"Give us this day our daily bread."

A. The Substance

1. The extent of the petition

The petition "give us this day our daily bread" isn't referring to a loaf of bread. Rather, it's talking about physical necessities. Now, man can't work on his spiritual life unless he is alive physically. It thrills me to know that the God of infinite celestial epochs, eternity, the planets, and the stars is the same God who cares for and meets my physical needs. He is concerned that I have food to eat, clothes to wear, and a place to rest. It thrills me to know that the infinite God of the universe takes care of our physical needs here on earth.

Martin Luther was right when he said in his smaller and larger catechisms on the Lord's Prayer that bread is the symbol for everything necessary for the preservation of this life, like food, a healthy body, good weather, house, home, wife, children, good government, and peace. The word *bread* in Matthew 6:11 refers to the physical necessities of life, not the luxuries. We can't use that verse to ask God for luxuries. What He chooses to give us in terms of luxury is by His grace. But He promises to give us necessities. Proverbs 30:8-9 reads, "Give me neither poverty nor riches; feed me with food convenient for me, lest I be full, and deny thee, and say, Who is the Lord? Or lest I be poor, and steal, and take the name of my God in vain." That is the same attitude reflected in Matthew 6:11. We aren't to be self-seeking, saying, "Give me more and more." Rather, we should say, "Lord, give me what I need."

2. The exercise of the petition

    You may think that we really don't have to pray for our physical needs, but we do. The petition, although it is not the desperate cry of a starving person, indicates that God promises to feed those who are righteous. He won't willfully withhold the provisions of life from a righteous person (Matt. 7:7-11). God will provide for the physical needs of any righteous person in any situation, within the purview of His will. Given that promise, some of us will still say, "The Lord will provide for me; why do I need to pray?" The petition in Matthew 6:11 is an affirmation that all our substance comes from God. When we say "give us this day our daily bread," we're saying, "God, I want to let You know that I realize You are the source of my life, food, shelter, and clothing."

    For example, why do I ask the Lord to forgive my sin and cleanse my life when He already promised to forgive my sin? Because He also said to keep on confessing my sin. When I say, "Lord, lead me in a certain direction," doesn't the Bible already say He will be my guide? Yes, but He also wants me to affirm that I recognize His leadership in my life. When I call out to the Lord and say, "Lord, hear and answer my prayer," don't I already know that He will and always has? Yes, but He wants me to affirm my confidence in Him because it exalts Him. Thus I may not have to say, "God, I don't have any food for my family. Where is it going to come from?" but I should always say, "Lord, everything I have and share with those whom I love comes from Your good and gracious hand." The petition in Matthew 6:11 is an affirmation that God is the source of everything. God cares about our physical needs. Although we may not always be on the edge of hunger, we are always to be thankful for everything God provides.

What Is the Primary Purpose of Eating?

The aim of the Disciples' Prayer is to glorify God. If you don't learn anything else from that prayer, remember that all your prayers are for God's glory. Thus when we say "give us this day our daily bread," our primary concern is not for our own sustenance but God's glory. In 1 Corinthians 10:31 Paul says, "Whether, therefore, ye eat, or drink, or whatever ye do, do all to the glory of God." How can eating food be to the glory of God? When you remember the source of your food and the capacity you have to enjoy it. Our eating will glorify God when we're thankful to Him for providing the nourishment we receive from it.

B. The Source

We tend to think that we provide everything for ourselves. We say, "I make my living. I earn my wages. I buy my bread. What do I owe God? I'm carrying my own load." We might not openly admit such things, but that attitude is often revealed by the way we act. When was the last time you said, "Lord, I thank You for my daily bread. I thank You for giving me food to eat, clothes to wear, and a shelter over my head. I thank you that I have a bed to rest in and that I have enough physical strength to know you, perceive you, and live life in a way that is rich and meaningful"? That's the attitude the Lord is talking about in Matthew 6:11.

1. The sovereign provider

God cares about the little things in our lives and in the world. He knows how many hairs you have on your head (Luke 12:7). The Lord knows and controls everything there is in this world. For that we are to be thankful.

Can Man Preserve the Earth?

We live in a day when people are fearful of mankind dying out because of the way we are polluting the world's resources. We're afraid of nuclear reactors ruining the environment, sewage polluting the rivers and lakes, overcrowding, smog, the destruction of the ozone layers around the earth, trash that's left in space, and chemicals that are getting into our bodies. Despite all the money and resources man has, he knows he is on the brink of devastating the environment to the point that he will have no more resources left. That ought to drive man to recognize that it is God who upholds everything. Man can't sustain the world.

According to the book of Revelation, there will come a day when God turns out the lights in the heavens (Matt. 24:29), turns rivers to blood (Rev. 16:4), and lets the sea swallow ships and destroy the fish (Rev. 8:8; 16:3). The world will be devastated. In Revelation 18 we read that the world economic system will collapse. All music will stop (Rev. 18:22). Everything will become worthless because there won't be anything left to purchase that is able to preserve life.

Man never considers that if it weren't for God's sustaining power, the world would fall apart. Even scientists realize that after all their calculations are done, there is an unknown element in the universe that makes everything hang together—and science doesn't even have a name for it. But Christians do.

Everything we have is from God. It is He who brings the rain to make things grow, causes the seasons to change, produces the minerals that make the soil fertile, provides the natural resources we use to propel ourselves around, and provides the materials from which we make our clothing. God made everything. Our daily bread—the necessities of physical life—are all from God. Thus, we should always say in our prayers, "God, give us this day our daily bread. We recognize You as the provider for all physical needs." Let's look more specifically at what God provides for us.

2. The specific provisions

    a) God provides food for us

    In Genesis 1:29-31, we read about how God has given us food: "God said, Behold, I have given you every herb bearing seed, which is upon the face of all the earth, and every tree, in which is the fruit of a tree yielding seed; to you it shall be for food. And to every beast of the earth, and to every fowl of the air, and to every thing that creepeth upon the earth, wherein there is life, I have given every green herb for food: and it was so. And God saw every thing that he had made, and, behold, it was very good."

    (1) The variety of foods

    God could have designed that we just eat mud for breakfast, lunch, and dinner. He could have made everything gray. But He is a God of marvelous variety. There are no two people who are

118

exactly alike. The number of colors in this world are almost unending. Likewise, there is great variety in the food we have. The key phrases in Genesis 1:29-31 are these: "God said, Behold, I have given you every herb bearing seed. . . . And to every beast of the earth, and to every fowl of the air, and to every thing that creepeth upon the earth . . . I have given every green herb for food. . . . And God saw every thing that he had made, and, behold, it was very good." God filled this world with wonder and variety, yet man corrupts that. Nonetheless, God gave us a variety of food that is good. He has graciously provided for us.

What Happened to the Jewish Dietary Laws?

There was a time when God gave special dietary laws to Israel, but He set them aside in Acts 10 and they no longer exist. He had given those laws so that the Israelites couldn't easily intermingle with the pagan nations around them and be corrupted. But because Israel stopped obeying God, the Lord set the nation aside and commissioned the church to do His work. At that time, the dietary laws were also set aside. Paul confirmed that when he said, "Let no man, therefore, judge you in food, or in drink" (Col. 2:16). But there are still people today who want to tell us there are certain things we can't eat. First Timothy 4 says, "In the latter times, some shall depart from the faith, giving heed to seducing spirits, and doctrines of demons . . . forbidding to marry, and commanding to abstain from foods, which God hath created to be received with thanksgiving by them who believe and know the truth" (vv. 1-3).

How Is Food Sanctified?

God has provided this incredible world of food for us so that we who believe and know the truth would express our thanks to Him. The rest of the world indulges itself without any gratitude at all. First Timothy 4:4-5 continues, "Every creature of God is good, and nothing is to be refused, if it is received with thanksgiving; for it is sanctified by the word of God and prayer." What does that mean? How did the food of the world become sanctified by the Word of God? Remember that in Genesis 1:31, God said everything was good. Thus, food was sanctified by Him. And how does food become sanctified by prayer? When it is received with thanksgiving. You sanctify food when you give thanks to God for it.

Do you really thank God for your food? You may say, "I wouldn't have a meal without praying beforehand." But for many of us, the prayer we give before we eat is usually quick and indifferent. We rattle them off to make sure the duty is done. Are you really thankful? Do you really see God as the source of everything? He has given us a marvelous variety of food, so we should be thankful. They have already been sanctified by the Word of God, and they are doubly sanctified when you say thanks to God. Saying thanks to God for His daily provisions that meet your physical needs fulfills the spirit of the petition "give us this day our daily bread." Realizing that God is the source of those provisions gives Him glory.

Have you ever stopped to think about all that God has given us to eat? Food is close to everyone's heart; every generation has seen it as an absolute necessity. But we often overlook the variety God has given us.

(*a*) Plant foods

    i) Grains

According to the Bible, the fields of Palestine produced wheat, barley, millet, and spelt (Ezek. 4:9). Although corn appears in the King James Version of the Bible, it's not referring to the corn known as Indian maize. The term *corn* was simply used as a general term for various cereal grains; the corn we have today was unknown to Palestine. These grains, according to Isaiah 3:1 and many other Bible passages, were crushed and made into a flour that would be used for making bread. Sometimes the kernels of grain were set on a stone to dry in the sun. Then the parched grains would be salted and used for snacks, much like the snack mixes you can get at health food stores today.

    ii) Nuts

In Genesis 43:11, we read that nuts were one of the foods available to the Israelites.

iii) Vegetables

As we look through Scripture, we find mention of cucumbers, melons, leeks (which are like onions), onions, garlic (Num. 11:5), beans, lentils (2 Sam. 17:28), bitter herbs (Ex. 12:8), mint, dill, cumin (Matt. 23:23), and sweet cane (Jer. 6:20), which may have been sugar cane. We all understand the important role sugar has in flavoring what we eat. Sugar, in its natural state, was made by the Lord.

iv) Fruits

The Bible speaks of grapes (Song of Sol. 2:13), raisins (1 Sam. 25:18), olives (Ex. 27:20), figs (Jer. 24:1), pomegranates (Ex. 28:33), apples (Prov. 25:11), and summer fruits (Jer. 40:10).

(b) Animal foods

i) Meat

There is nothing wrong with eating meat. It's not more spiritual to be a vegetarian. If you prefer to be a vegetarian, that's fine. And if you want to eat meat, that's all right too. Whether we eat meat or not isn't a biblical issue.

God provided oxen, sheep, and goats for Israel (Lev. 22:27). The restriction from pork was removed in Acts 10. Also available was lamb (2 Sam. 12:4), stalled ox (an ox kept in a stall so its muscles couldn't become tough; Prov. 15:17), and fattened calves (1 Sam. 28:24). There were seven types of game that could be hunted for food (Deut. 14:5), as well as fish (Neh. 13:16) and four types of insects (Lev. 11:22). I don't know how they served those insects; it's possible they were eaten with their nuts and grains. There were different kinds of fowl, such as partridges (1 Sam. 26:20), quail (Ex. 16:13), pigeons and turtledoves (Lev. 12:6), and chickens (Matt. 23:37).

ii) Dairy products

There was milk (Deut. 32:14) and the by-products of milk, which included curds or butter (Gen. 18:8), cheese (Job 10:10), and eggs from their chickens (Isa. 10:14). The milk mainly came from cows, goats, and sheep, although there was also camel milk.

(c) Condiments

The Lord also provided condiments for flavoring food. They include honey, sugar from sweet cane, salt, mint, anise, cumin, and mustard seeds.

(2) The vast amount of foods

God has provided us with an incredible abundance of food. In fact, when God told the Israelites about the Promised Land, He told them they were going into a land of milk and honey (Deut. 6:3). In other words, God was saying that the land possessed a bounty of physical necessities. If you go to Israel today, you'll see that description is true. Israel has some of the most fertile land in the world, and God knew that when He sent His people there. God created an incredible, abundant variety of the things needed to meet our physical needs.

There are some illustrations in the Old Testament that give us an idea of how much food there really was in Israel. In 1 Samuel 25:18, a woman named Abigail put together "two hundred loaves [of bread], and two skins of wine, and five sheep ready dressed, and five measures of parched grain, and an hundred clusters of raisins, and two hundred cakes of figs, and laid them on asses." In 2 Samuel 16:1, 1 Kings 4:22-23, and other Scripture verses appear more lists of food in abundance. Where did it all come from? God. He made everything. Now He didn't make hamburgers or hot dogs, but everything is made up of component parts of what God made.

b) God provides clothing for us

We depend on animals and plants for our clothing. Some people might say, "I have clothes that are made from polyester, which doesn't originate from animals or plants." But polyester comes from a petroleum product, which comes from the earth.

Every element of everything that we eat, wear, or use in our homes came from the earth, which God made. Not to recognize that daily is the height of indifference and ingratitude. God is active daily in upholding His world so that it supports our physical needs. We should be grateful for God's gracious, loving provision.

c) God provides food for the plants and animals

God has set up an incredibly complex network to support the ecological system on this earth. To provide food for man, He also has to feed the plants and animals that feed man. The minerals in the soil feed plants, and those plants and some animals feed other animals. God provides plant eaters with herbage, oxen with grass and straw, horses with barley, birds with seeds, and locusts with plants. God keeps the whole cycle going.

Something else that keeps the plants and animals alive, as well as man, is rain. That too is a gift from God. If He shut off the heavens, nothing would grow. If there were no grass or plants, the animals wouldn't be able to eat—and neither would we. Eventually, everything would die. So God upholds the ecological system through rain.

Everything that we have is from God's hand. Some people might say, "Wait a minute. *I* earn my money." To them we should cite Deuteronomy 8:18, which says, "It is [God] who giveth thee power to get wealth." It is God who gave you the capacity to bend your back, open your mouth, talk, think, and make a living. Even the money you get from the bank was made from materials God created. The paper came from trees and the coins came from minerals.

There is nothing in the world that God didn't create. We are utterly dependent upon God's provision. First Chronicles 29:14 says, "All things come of thee, and of thine own have we given thee." Anything you give back to God is something He originally gave to you.

Thomas Watson, a great Puritan with a heart for God, wrote this "If all be a gift, see the odious ingratitude of men who sin against their giver! God feeds them, and they fight against him; he gives them bread, and they give him insults. How unworthy is this Should we not cry shame of him who had a friend always feeding him with money, and yet he should betray and injure him? Thus ungratefully do sinners deal with God; they not only forget his mercies, but abuse them. 'When I had fed them to the full, they then committed adultery.' Oh, how horrid is it to sin against a bountiful God!—to strike the hands that relieve us!" (*The Lord's Prayer* [London: Banner of Truth Trust, 1972], p. 197).

In Deuteronomy 32:15, we read of one to whom God gave abundantly: "Jeshurun [Israel] grew fat, and kicked. . . . Then he forsook God who made him." With some people, the more they have, the less grateful they become. We need to make sure that doesn't happen to us. I think such a warning would apply to those of us with many material goods more than it would to those who have very little, because the latter tend to express gratitude for their daily bread. We often forget the petition in Matthew 6:11 because we have too much. Yet we are ever dependent on God for everything we have. It is He who gives us our physical supply. The next time you pray, remember to affirm that all your physical needs are met by Him. And ask Him to continue providing for you so that His name might be glorified in your prayer of thanksgiving.

Focusing on the Facts

1. Why does the petition "give us this day our daily bread" seem so remote to many of us (see p. 110)?
2. Does the section of the Disciples' Prayer dealing with man's needs set God aside? Explain (see p. 112).
3. How do some people approach prayer (see p. 113)?
4. Describe the dimensions of life that are encompassed in the last three petitions in the Disciples' Prayer (Matt. 6:11-13; see p. 114).
5. Prayer is not used to_____God and make Him _____ His _____ (see p. 114).
6. To what does the word *bread* in Matthew 6:11 refer (see p. 115)?
7. What promise of God is affirmed in the petition for our daily bread (see p. 116)?
8. Why should we pray for our daily provisions even if we're sure God will provide for us (see p. 116)?

9. What should be our primary concern when we say "give us this day our daily bread" (see p. 117)?
10. What attitude should we have regarding the physical provisions God grants us (see p. 117)?
11. According to Genesis 1:29-31, what did God provide on the earth, and for whom did He provide it (see pp. 118-19)?
12. Why did God designate special dietary laws for the Old Testament Israelites? What happened to those laws (see p. 119)?
13. Explain how food becomes sanctified (see p. 119).
14. Mention the variety of grains, vegetables, and fruits that were found in Palestine (see pp. 120-21).
15. What are some of the animals and dairy products that were available to the Israelites as food (see pp. 121-22)?
16. What did God mean when He said that the Promised Land was a land of milk and honey (Deut. 6:3; see p. 122)?
17. Every element of everything that we _____, _____, or _____ came from the earth, which _____ made (see p. 123).
18. Describe some of the things God does to uphold the ecological system in our world (see p. 123).
19. What do Deuteronomy 8:18 and 1 Chronicles 29:14 say to us (see pp. 123-24)?
20. What do we need to make sure never happens to us (see p. 124)?

Pondering the Principles

1. What would you say to someone who says we have the right to demand favors from God? For ideas on what you might say in your answer, consider what you have learned in this lesson and also look up Matthew 6:19-34 and James 4:3.

2. Read Proverbs 30:8-9. Is that the attitude you have toward God when you pray? What do you think are some of the causes of discontentment in a Christian? What are some things a Christian can do to learn to be content with what God has given him? Take some time now to write down a list of the physical provisions God has given you in the last two or three months, and thank Him for meeting your needs.

3. Many of us get into the habit of saying quick or meaningless prayers before we eat. How would you describe your prayers at such times? Do they vary in content? What is generally your attitude when you say them? Is there anything you can do to make those prayers more pleasing to the Lord? When we truly

thank God for the food He has provided for us, we will enjoy it more.

4. God promises to provide for us the basic necessities of life. Anything He provides in the way of luxuries is by His grace. Sometimes it's possible for us to want a luxury badly enough to see it as a need when it really isn't. To avoid doing that, look up the definitions of the word *luxury* and the word *necessity*. Memorize those definitions. Always work to keep the differences between the two clear in your mind.

8
The Provision of Prayer—Part 2

Outline

Introduction

Review
I. God's Paternity (v. 9a)
II. God's Priority (v. 9b)
II. God's Program (v. 10a)
V. God's Plan (v. 10b)
V. God's Provision (v. 11)
  A. The Substance
  B. The Source

Lesson
  C. The Supplication
    1. The promise of provision
    2. The picture of provision
      a) The prosperity of America
      b) The poverty of India
        (1) The loss of resources for human needs
          (a) To cows
          (b) To mice
        (2) The loss of regard for human life
    3. The preoccupation with provisions
      a) The distraction of physical necessities
      b) The devotion to spiritual necessities
    4. The pattern of provision
      a) Through our own efforts
      b) Through the generosity of others
  D. The Seekers
  E. The Schedule
    1. The element of time
    2. The exercise of trust

Introduction

In Matthew 6:9-13, Jesus contrasts His standard of prayer with that of the scribes and Pharisees. The contrast, to sum it up in a simple statement, is that Jesus' standard of prayer focused on God while the religious leaders' prayers focused on themselves. In Matthew 6:5 Christ says, "They love to pray standing in the synagogues and at the corners of the streets, that they may be seen by men." In verse 7 He says in effect, "They use vain repetitions just like the pagans do, as if they could cajole God into giving them what they want." Verse 8 indicates that the scribes and Pharisees prayed as if they had some information to give to God that was not at His disposal. Their prayers focused entirely on themselves, so Christ told them, "When you pray, you are to focus on God."

All prayer is to focus on God. Prayer is not primarily for us; it's for Him. It's not a vehicle for my gain but for God's glory. The first three petitions of the prayer, "hallowed be thy name," "thy kingdom come," and "thy will be done on earth," indicate that our perspective is to be on God first. No petitions regarding ourselves appear until that is done. And anything that we do ask for is to hallow God's name, bring His kingdom to earth, and be an expression of His will.

Review

As we continue our study of the Disciples' Prayer, we have moved from the petitions related directly to God to those related to human need. The petition we are currently looking at in verse 11 says, "Give us this day our daily bread."

I. GOD'S PATERNITY (v. 9a; see pp. 22-31)

II. GOD'S PRIORITY (v. 9b; see pp. 36-49)

III. GOD'S PLAN (v. 10a; see pp. 59-69)

IV. GOD'S PURPOSE (v. 10b; see pp. 77-87, 94-107)

V. GOD'S PROVISION (v. 11)

"Give us this day our daily bread."

A. The Substance (see pp. 115-17)

What is the substance we request from God? Our daily bread. The concept of bread in that verse is really a symbol for all our physical needs. That encompasses the basic needs of food, clothing, and shelter—the basic necessities of life. We are of little use to God in accomplishing His goals if He doesn't meet our basic physical needs and keep us alive.

B. The Source (see pp. 117-24)

The petition for our daily bread assumes that the source is God. That is implied in the phrase "give us." We look to God as the source of everything. Everything you possess, He provided. He is the Creator, Sustainer, and Preserver of the entire universe. Everything that we have is from His hand.

The first petition that rises from the heart of a child of God concerning himself is one that speaks of physical need. There is nothing wrong with seeking God in regard to that, as long as it is done with the motive that through His provision His name will be hallowed, His kingdom will come, and His will be done. God desires to meet our physical needs. James 1:17 says, "Every good gift and every perfect gift is from above, and cometh down from the Father of lights, with whom is no variableness, neither shadow of turning." We know from 1 Timothy 4 that everything is to be "received with thanksgiving; for it is sanctified by the word of God and prayer" (vv. 4-5). God has given us everything good to enjoy.

The petition "give us this day our daily bread" is not the prayer of a beggar. Although it could be prayed by someone who has nothing for his next meal, it is primarily an acknowledgment that God is the source of every physical provision. Some people might pray, "Lord, I don't have anything to eat for my next meal. I ask You to give me my daily bread that You may be glorified in the provision." Others of us might say, "Lord, You have supplied so much, and I thank You for doing so. I acknowledge You as the source and ask that You continue to provide with such graciousness so that Your name might be glorified." Whichever way you state that prayer, the petition still recognizes God as the source of all physical provisions.

Lesson

C. The Supplication

1. The promise of provision

What right do we have to ask God for our daily bread? Is there some basis on which that petition is valid? Yes. God has promised to meet our physical needs. If He made that promise, then we have a right to ask Him to fulfill it. There are some passages that I hope will help you to understand how God desires to meet your physical needs. As we look them over, keep in mind that He is not bound to meet everyone's physical needs. There are some conditions to His provision.

a) Psalm 37

    (1) A word for the righteous

Verse 3 says, "Trust in the Lord, and do good." That simple statement is profound because it encompasses the significance of salvation. When we believe God, the result is good works. James 2:26 says that faith without works is dead. So simply saying, "Trust in the Lord, and do good" is like summing up soteriology, the doctrine of salvation. Now, what promise is extended to those whose belief is manifest? Psalm 37:3 continues, "So shalt thou dwell in the land, and verily thou shalt be fed."

Isn't that a great promise? Although the promises in the Bible have much to do with spiritual truth, they don't exclude the physical aspect of life. We would be of little spiritual good to the Lord if He didn't meet our physical needs. One passage that refers to both the spiritual and physical aspects of our lives is 2 Corinthians 9. Verse 7 tells us that we are to give "not grudgingly, or of necessity; for God loveth a cheerful giver." We are to sow not sparingly but bountifully (v. 6). As a result, God will "both minister bread for your food, and multiply your seed sown, and increase the fruits of your righteousness" (v. 10). When you invest in God's kingdom, He will not only provide spiritual fruit but also bread for food. God's physical provision is a biblical promise.

    (2) A warning for the wicked

Continuing through Psalm 37, this is what we read concerning God's provision: "Delight thyself also in the Lord. . . . Commit thy way unto the Lord" (vv. 4-5). Verses 7-9 say, "Rest in the Lord. . . .Cease from anger, and forsake wrath. . . . For evildoers shall be cut off." Verse 13 says of the wicked, "The Lord shall laugh at him; for he seeth that his day is coming."

In verses 18-19 David writes, "The Lord knoweth the days of the upright, and their inheritance shall be forever. They shall not be ashamed in the evil time; and in the days of famine they shall be satisified." God promises to provide for His own, even when there is famine. The unrighteous will perish, and the righteous will have provision. Verse 20 continues, "The wicked shall perish, and the enemies of the Lord shall be like the fat of lambs. They shall consume; into smoke shall they consume away." Lamb fat burns rapidly, and that's how the wicked will perish. God has no obligation to provide for them. He provides only for His own. That's not to say we will always be feasting. Proverbs 15:17 says, "Better is a dinner of herbs where love is, than a stalled ox and hatred therewith." When our relationship with God is right, our food doesn't have to be fancy.

Don't ever forget that God is concerned for our physical provision and that we can claim those provisions at His good and gracious hand. Psalm 37:22-24 says that the righteous "are blessed by [God and] shall inherit the earth; and they who are cursed by him shall be cut off. The steps of a good man are ordered by the Lord, and he delighteth in his way. Though he fall, he shall not be utterly cast down; for the Lord upholdeth him with his hand." The message in those verses is that a righteous man is cared for by the Lord. We come to the climax in verse 25, where King David says, "I have been young, and now am old; yet have I not seen the righteous forsaken, nor his seed begging bread." Why is that? Verse 26 gives us the answer: "[God] is ever merciful, and lendeth; and his seed is blessed." That's a good reason for us to heed verse 27: "Depart from evil, and do good." God feeds those who belong to Him.

b) Jonah 4

In verse 6, we read that God provided a gourd plant to shade Jonah.

c) Luke 18

Christ said, "There is no man that hath left house, or parents, or brethren, or wife, or children, for the kingdom of God's sake, who shall not receive manifold more in this present time, and in the age to come life everlasting" (vv. 29-30). God has provided the homes, land, fathers, and mothers of those who are His own, and He will continue to provide for us in the life to come.

It is tremendous to know that God has promised to meet our physical needs. Those who don't know God have no such claim on Him. He might feed the unrighteous on occasion by His gracious and sovereign choice, but He's not bound to that. Someday, all those who are wicked will go hungry. Luke 6:25 says, "Woe to you who are well-fed now, for you shall be hungry" (NASB*). God is bound only to the physical provision of those who are His children.

Will the Earth Run Out of Food?

In India, men forsake their wives and their children just to find food. Families commit suicide together. Mothers throw their babies into the swirling waters of the Ganges River as sacrifices to the gods because they think there is more religious virtue in having them die as a sacrifice rather than from malnutrition. But even with all the famines and starving people in the world, the issue isn't whether the earth can provide enough food. Former Prime Minister Indira Gandhi said that there are enough resources in India to feed the entire nation and feed others beside [Detroit News, 8 February 1971], p. A-20).

Some people think the world can't produce enough food for mankind, but that's not true. I read that the more people there are in the world, the more productivity there will be because man is a productive being. I also learned that you could fit the entire population of the world into the state of Montana. That would leave a lot of open space. Only about 15 percent of all harvestable land is used. So the problem isn't a lack of resources or an overabundance of people. In fact, there are less people per square mile in New York today than there were fifty years ago (statistics from Robert L. Sassone, Handbook on Population, 3d ed., 1973 report to the California legislature; Julian L. Simon, The Ultimate Resource [Princeton, N.J.: Princeton U., 1981]).

We have the resources to produce enough food for everyone, but what ultimately cuts people off from those resources is a spiritual matter. Those who don't acknowledge God will lack provisions. God promises to provide for His own, and He made a world that can provide for everyone if they would just turn to Him.

*New American Standard Bible.

d) Psalm 33

The psalmist wrote, "Behold, the eye of the Lord is upon those who fear him, upon those who hope in his mercy, to deliver their soul from death, and to keep them alive in famine" (vv. 18-19). It's amazing to me that God would sort out His own people in the midst of a famine and preserve them. It's not likely that we will be miraculously fed by ravens or angels (1 Kings 17:4; Matt. 4:11) or have a gourd grow over our heads (Jonah 4:6), but God will feed His people. He will take care of them in the midst of famine.

e) Psalm 34

David said, "Oh, fear the Lord, ye his saints; for there is no lack to them that fear him. The young lions do lack, and suffer hunger; but they who seek the Lord shall not lack any good thing" (vv. 9-10).

f) Proverbs 3

This exhortation is given to us in verses 5-6: "Trust in the Lord with all thine heart, and lean not unto thine own understanding. In all thy ways acknowledge him, and he shall direct thy paths." What is the result of doing that? Verses 8-10 say, "It shall be health to thy navel, and marrow to thy bones. Honor the Lord with thy substance, and with the first fruits of all thine increase; so shall thy barns be filled with plenty, and thy presses shall burst out with new wine." God provides for our physical needs in His gracious care as a loving Father.

g) Proverbs 10

Verse 3 says, "The Lord will not suffer the soul of the righteous to famish, but he casteth away the substance of the wicked." It is abundantly clear in Scripture that God is committed to the care of His people.

h) Matthew 7

Jesus said, "Ask, and it shall be given you; seek, and ye shall find; knock, and it shall be opened unto you" (v. 7). Now that verse is usually tied to the idea of someone coming to Christ and asking for salvation. But we gain a better understanding of what Christ was saying by reading verses 8-11: "For every one that asketh receiveth; and he that seeketh findeth; and to him that knocketh it shall be opened. Or what man is there of you whom, if his son ask bread, will he give him a stone? Or if he ask a fish, will he give him a serpent? If ye then, being evil, know how to give good gifts unto your children, how much more shall your Father, who is in heaven, give good things to them that ask him?" What good things did Jesus talk about in His illustration? Bread and meat. God is concerned with giving the basics of life to His people, just as a father would provide for his child.

i)   Matthew 6

Verses 25-34 of this chapter tell us to not worry about what we eat, drink, or wear. God will take care of those things. Our priority is to seek first the kingdom of God. Everything else will find its rightful place as a result.

There have been times when God has done supernatural miracles in caring for those who are His own, but He usually meets our needs through other Christians. Where there is a Christian community, there will be a caring for one another. Because a child of God has such a high view of the value of man, he seeks not only to meet his own needs but also the needs of others. For example, James 2:15-16 says that "if a brother or sister be naked, and destitute of daily food, and one of you say unto them, Depart in peace, be ye warmed and filled," then it's questionable whether that person is truly saved. First John 3:17 says, "Whosoever hath this world's good, and seeth his brother have need, and shutteth up his compassions from him, how dwelleth the love of God in him?" It is the innate response of one who knows God that he supply the needs of others in addition to caring for his own needs.

2.   The picture of provision

The fact that God provides for His own is illustrated to us all around the globe. Where there is a Christian heritage and a high view of human life, there is much in the way of provisions. But in the parts of the world where there are no Christian roots and a low view of human life, there is usually great famine and impoverishment. Generally, nations that have been under the influence of the gospel and Christian teaching have a high respect for the value of man as created in God's image and as the object of divine redemption. Such nations are not as prone to suffer hunger and deprivation as are nations without Christian roots. There may be some exceptions to that rule but not very many.

a)   The prosperity of America

America is a nation founded on Christian principles. Christianity is what gave this country a high view of human life. Christian principles are reflected in the Bill of Rights. Today, we're still concerned with minimum wage laws, equality for everyone, equal educational opportunities, and equal pay for equal work. We're concerned that everyone has medical care, and we have a welfare system that provides for those who don't have jobs. Where did those concerns come from? But as Christian values weaken, new ideas creep in. Abortionists promote the mass murder of unborn babies, and advocates of euthanasia want to allow for the elimination of those who are a burden to society. Some want to decide who gets born to whom. Those attitudes do not reflect a high view of man.

America, in the midst of its atheism, humanism, immorality, and departure from Christian truth, still can't remove completely the residual impact of the high view of man that came from the Bible, even though many would deny that's where the view came from. The ungodly people of our nation, according to 1 Corinthians 7:14, are sanctified by the presence of believers. They receive the benefits associated with the presence of Christians.

b)   The poverty of India

India, which is probably one of the most influential nations in the world and the birthplace of Hinduism, serves as a contrast to America. Hinduism basically spawned all the religions that engulf the Orient. It is the source of Buddhism, Jainism, Sikhism, and many mystical cults. Hinduism is still the main religion in India, and the entire legacy of Hinduism in the Orient is deprivation. The view of man is low; he is not seen as being created in God's image. In fact, the Hindus believe their gods are all sinful.

135

The natural resources of India can meet the needs of her people, but the people's religion has trapped them from using those resources. Six out of ten people in Calcutta live on the streets without food, shelter, or adequate clothing. The total population in India is about 660 million people. Fifteen million of them die every year, and 27 million are born. With that many new people each year, more and more end up living on the streets. Is that because there isn't enough food? No. The problem is understood better when one examines the religious system there.

(1) The loss of resources for human needs

    (*a*) To cows

> There are about 330 million deities in India. The one supreme deity is known by three names, depending on how he manifests himself: Vishnu, Brahma, and Shiva. But below him are a plethora of gods. Those gods are personified in the cows of India. The Hindus believe cows are incarnate gods. That's where the phrase "sacred cow" comes from. Also, everything that comes from a cow is considered sacred, including the dung and urine. It's not unusual to see pious, low-caste Hindus on the streets catching cow urine and sipping it. And to kill or eat a cow is thought to be worse than cannibalism.

> The cows eat about 20 percent of India's food supply. (The cows live long because they have rest homes for those that stop giving milk!) Every cow eats enough food to feed seven people, and there are about 200 million cows in India. All together, the cows eat enough food to feed more than one billion people. If none of the food produced in India were given to those cows, there would be enough food not only for the people living in India, but also the continents of Antarctica, Australia, Africa, and Europe (*Los Angeles Herald-Examiner* [21 November 1971]; *Detroit News* [8 February 1972].

(*b*) To mice

About 15 percent of the food supply in India is eaten by mice, which are not killed because people fear they might be killing someone in that stage of reincarnation. A person attains "salvation" in Hinduism by reaching *nirvana*, a state where he is no longer reincarnated. So they believe every living being is at some stage in the reincarnation cycle. That explains the caste (class) system in India. Everyone wants to attain a higher caste the next time he is born. If he does bad things in his current life, he might drop down into the animal kingdom, which has 84,000 levels. Every animal is believed to be someone reincarnated on his way up or down the scale. To kill an animal would alter the cycle of *karma* and push someone into another life not intended for him. You'll also become an animal yourself in your next life.

(2) The loss of regard for human life

The social effects of the belief in reincarnation are beyond description. If you see a destitute, wretched person, you are not to meet his need. The only way that person will be able to get out of his destitute level is to do penance in this life at that particular level. If you help out such a person, you relieve him of the penalty he is supposed to pay, and when he dies, he won't ascend to the next level of reincarnation. Thus, there is no regard for human life at all. A typical Hindu response to a beggar is, "I wonder what you did to deserve this? I hope you can work your way out of this situation" (*Encyclopaedia Britannica*, vol. 8, pp. 888-908; *Eerdman's Handbook to World Religions* [Grand Rapids: Eerdmans, 1982]).

India has suffered deprivation not because of a lack of food but because of its religious system. Without a Christian heritage or the influence of God's power as a result of the presence of believers, a country will not have a proper view of man as created in the image of God. The Lord feeds His people and feeds those who are around His people. Apart from belonging to Him, there is no guarantee of physical supply.

The problems with lack of physical provisions in the world are not the result of a lack of resources. I don't believe those who say that someday the world will run out of food. What we do know is that many of those who don't know God, who is the source of all food, will lack food.

3. The preoccupation with provisions

    a) The distraction of physical necessities

    In Matthew 6:11, Jesus puts a limit on self-focused prayers with the statement "give us this day our daily bread." We don't need to spend a lot of time thinking about our physical needs. God doesn't want us to be preoccupied with the physical. That is the lowest level of human need. God was saying He would take care of our needs. In Matthew 6:25 Jesus says, "Therefore, I say unto you, Be not anxious for your life, what ye shall eat, or what ye shall drink; nor yet for your body, what ye shall put on." Why? God takes care of the birds (v. 26), the lilies (vv. 28-29), and the grass (v. 30). Thus we are told in verses 31-32, "Be not anxious saying, What shall we eat? or, What shall we drink? or, With what shall we be clothed? For after all these things do the Gentiles seek. For your heavenly Father knoweth that ye have need of all these things." God knows that He must supply our physical needs; they will be taken care of. Verse 33 concludes, "Seek ye first the kingdom of God, and his righteousness, and all these things shall be added unto you." Let God take care of your physical needs, and focus on spiritual things.

    b) The devotion to spiritual necessities

    In Colossians 3:2 Paul says, "Set your affection on things above, not on things on the earth." God wants us to acknowledge Him as the source of all provision so that we can focus our lives on investing in the kingdom and the matter of righteousness. The people of the world seek after physical needs, but Christians don't need to because God promises to provide for them.

4. The pattern of provision

   a) Through our own efforts

   Genesis 3:19 describes the primary way our needs are taken care of: Man will earn his bread by the sweat of his face. So we're not supposed to say, "I'm spiritual. I'll wait until God sends some ravens to feed me." Nor should we say, "God, grow a gourd to give me some shade." Instead, we are to have a high enough value of ourselves before God to be obedient to Him and to work so that we can feed and clothe ourselves. We are to work, not just sit around. In fact, 1 Timothy 5:8 says, "If any provide not for his own, and specially for those of his own house, he . . . is worse than an infidel."

   We are to be committed to work. In 2 Thessalonians 3:10-12 Paul says, "When we were with you, this we commanded you, that if any would not work, neither should he eat. For we hear that there are some who walk among you disorderly, working not at all but are busybodies. Now them that are such we command and exhort, by our Lord Jesus Christ, that with quietness they work, and eat their own bread."

   b) Through the generosity of others

   There are some people who are unable to work, and we should meet their needs as well. Paul's heart went out to the poor saints in Jerusalem. They had such great need that he traveled all over Asia Minor collecting money for them (Rom. 15:26; 2 Cor. 8-9). He was energetically involved in collecting money to meet the needs of poor people, yet at the same time he had no sympathy for someone who was poor simply because he was unwilling to work.

Will God Allow a Christian to Die of Starvation?

It's wonderful to know that God is going to supply our physical needs. Yet there are some who will say, "What about all the people in Hebrews 11 who had such great faith? They were saints of the highest order of whom the world was not worthy. They were persecuted, slaughtered, and often without food, shelter, and clothing. Doesn't that contradict what you've been saying?" No, because God supplies our needs only until it's time for us to die. One way He may choose for us to go home to Him is through a lack of provision. But until that time in His sovereign plan, your needs will be met. Only God knows the specific dimension of what those needs are. He takes care of our physical needs until we die, and then we enter into an abundance that's inconceivable.

An analogy could be made using Matthew 18:10, which tells us that children have angels who are before the Father and watching over their every need. Some people ask, "Is it true that children have guardian angels?" It may be true based on Matthew 18:10. If so, then does that mean the guardian angel was asleep on the job when a child dies? No, because the angel fulfills his function only until the sovereignty of God deems that life should end. God is saying in essence, "MacArthur, you have only so much time in My sovereign plan, and I've called you to a specific task. If you set your heart and mind on My kingdom and righteousness, I will meet your physical needs." Thus, my preoccupation is not to be with the physical. When the Lord sees fit to remove the physical protection I receive, then I will leave this world and enter into a fullness of existence in the next world that will give me a supply of eternal resources that I couldn't even dream of.

So when we say "give us this day our daily bread" what are we saying? We are trusting God to supply all the physical necessities of our lives. We are affirming that because we are His children and are walking in submission to His righteous will, we know that He will take care of our physical needs. We are to lift up our hearts in gratitude and set our affections on things above (Col. 3:2).

D. The Seekers

Who are the seekers of daily bread? *We* are. Notice that the petition says "give *us*" (emphasis added). Those of us in Christ's church are not isolated from one another. The use of the plural precludes all selfishness in our prayers. The phrase "give us" embodies the entire Christian community. No believer will have an abundance of necessities if he knows a brother in Christ who has less than enough. The petition for our daily bread encompasses the concept of sharing.

E. The Schedule

1. The element of time

How often will God give us our daily bread? Matthew 6:11 says, "This day." God will provide bread for the coming day. That is a simple, beautiful way of saying, "One day at a time, Father, I accept Your provision." It stresses the contentment that comes when we live with a day-by-day confidence in God and don't worry about the future.

2. The exercise of trust

Most Christians who worry do so over things that haven't yet happened. That shows they are not sure God will provide their daily bread in the future. They are doubting His promise. I'm not saying we shouldn't have money or goods put aside in case we are hit by hard times. We are to be like the ant in Proverbs 6:6-8 and plan for the future. The petition in Matthew 6:11 reminds us to ask only for physical provisions for this day only and not worry about tomorrow (cf. Matt. 6:34).

Prayer focuses on God as the One who supplies. It acknowledges that He is the source of all our physical needs, and it teaches us to live one day at a time in the confidence that He will meet those needs. I trust that as we pray every day, we will remember to focus on spiritual matters because we know God is graciously caring for our physical needs. Don't get bogged down with thoughts about physical necessities. Don't lose your joy by getting wrapped up in mundane things. Set your affections on things above. Seek first the kingdom, and let God take care of the rest.

Many people today talk about helping the poor and feeding the hungry. That's a good and necessary cause. But I also believe it's better to give someone the gospel than to give him food. If you give a man food, he will be hungry again tomorrow. But if you give him the gospel of Christ, God will take care of Him throughout eternity. One thing we can promise every unbeliever is that God will take them under His watchful care as a loving Father when they enter into a relationship with His Son. That's a glorious truth.

Focusing on the Facts

1. On what basis is the petition for our daily bread valid (see p. 129)?
2. What promise is given to those who trust in the Lord (Ps. 37:3; see p. 130)?
3. What will God do in response when we invest in His kingdom (2 Cor. 9:10; see p. 130)?
4. What great truth does David state in Psalm 37:25-26 (see p. 131)?
5. For whom is God not obligated to provide (Luke 6:25; see p. 132)?
6. Discuss why the problems of famine and starvation aren't necessarily related to a lack of resources (see p. 132).

7. Explain the significance of the words in Matthew 7:7-11 (see pp. 133-34).
8. Explain the relationship between an abundance of resources and religious roots (see pp. 134-35).
9. What indicates that America has a high view of man (see p. 135)?
10. What legacy has Hinduism brought to the Orient (see p. 135)?
11. Give two of the reasons for the poverty of India (see pp. 136-37).
12. What view do people in India have toward those who are destitute (see p. 137)?
13. Ultimately, why has India suffered deprivation (see p. 137)?
14. What are we commanded to do in Colossians 3:2? Explain (see p. 138).
15. Describe two ways in which it is possible for us to obtain the physical provisions we need (see p. 139).
16. Will God allow a Christian to die of starvation (see pp. 139-40)?
17. The petition for our daily bread _____ the concept of _____ (see p. 140).
18. Explain the significance of the phrase "this day" in Matthew 6:11 (see p. 140).
19. Why is it better to give a poor man the gospel than to give him food (see p. 141)?

Pondering the Principles

1. The Bible clearly affirms that God has committed Himself to meeting our physical needs. How has He provided for you and your family? Can you think of specific provisions you have received in the past where you could see God's hand involved in the situation? How has God used you to meet the needs of others? What are some things you could be doing now that would help to meet the needs of others? Thank God for how He has provided for you, and start developing a habit of searching for ways you can provide for others.

2. Here is a fun project you can do with your family that will help you to visualize the extent of God's provision for mankind. Write down the names of some of the vegetables and fruits that you purchase from your local market. Starting with the planting of seeds in the ground, name everything that is involved in the growth of those fruits and vegetables. Discuss what God has done to ensure that those products can continue to be raised, and thank Him for providing them all.

3. Read Matthew 6:19-21 and Colossians 3:2. How much do you

focus on physical necessities as compared to spiritual concerns? Is there evidence in your life that you are laying up treasures here on earth? What actions in your life show that you are investing in God's kingdom? Compare your answers to those two questions and determine what they reveal about your priorities. What are some ways you can focus more on advancing God's kingdom and setting your affections on things above? When you evaluate where you are putting your treasures, it is helpful and encouraging to keep in mind the infinite abundance we will know when we dwell with Christ in His eternal kingdom.

9
The Pardon of Prayer—Part 1

Outline

Introduction
A. The Erasure of Sin
B. The Effects of Sin

Review
I. God's Paternity (v. 9*a*)
II. God's Priority (v. 9*b*)
III. God's Program (v. 10*a*)
IV. God's Plan (v. 10*b*)
V. God's Provision (v. 11)

Lesson
VI. God's Pardon (vv. 12, 14-15)
  A. The Problem—Sin
    1. The width of sin
    2. The work of sin
      a) It dominates man's life
      b) It brings man under Satan's control
      c) It brings man under God's wrath
      d) It subjects man to misery
    3. The words for sin
      a) *Hamartia*
      b) *Parabasis*
      c) *Anomia*
      d) *Paraptōma*
      e) *Opheilēma*
    4. The wages of sin
  B. The Provision—Forgiveness
    1. The clarification about forgiveness
    2. The categories of forgiveness
      a) Judicial forgiveness

(1) The pronouncement
(2) The payment
(3) The purification

Introduction

The petition that appears in Matthew 6:12, which is a part of the Disciples' Prayer, is this: "Forgive us our debts, as we forgive our debtors." Verses 14-15 act as a footnote to that petition: "If ye forgive men their trespasses, your heavenly Father will also forgive you; but if ye forgive not men their trespasses, neither will your Father forgive your trespasses." Those three verses are the theme of this lesson.

A. The Erasure of Sin

The focus of Matthew 6:12 is on sin and its forgiveness. That is a petition every person needs to include in his prayer life. We don't think enough about the fact that the most essential, blessed, and difficult thing God ever did was to provide forgiveness for man's sins. It is most essential because it keeps us from eternal hell and gives us joy even in this life. It is most blessed because it introduces us into a fellowship with God that goes on forever. And it is most difficult because it cost the Son of God His life. Forgiveness of sin is the greatest need of the human heart.

B. The Effects of Sin

Sin has a twofold effect. Its future effect is that it damns men forever, and its present effect is that it robs men of fullness of life by bringing upon their consciences unrelieved guilt. Thus, it is unquestionably the major problem in the life of man, and it needs a solution.

When sin is unforgiven, the guilt and condemnation carried by the conscience has a definite effect. Shakespeare, even though he wasn't a theologian, knew that people can become sick in their minds and bodies from unconfessed and unforgiven sin. In his play *Macbeth*, he wrote of the struggle and anxiety Lady Macbeth had in her heart as a result of helping to murder King Duncan I of Scotland. She took on all kinds of psychosomatic disorders as a result of the un-confessed murder. She called for a physician to visit her, and he told Macbeth, "Not so sick, my lord, as she is troubled with thick-coming fancies, that keep her from her rest." Macbeth responded, "Canst thou not minister to a mind diseased, pluck from the memory a rooted sorrow, raze out the written troubles of the brain, and with some sweet oblivious antidote cleanse the stuff'd bosom of that perilous stuff which weighs upon the heart?" (Act V.iii.34).

Psychiatrist William Sadler said that a clean conscience is a great step toward barricading the mind against neuroticism (*Mental Mischief and Emotional Conflicts* [St. Louis: Mosley, 1947]). John R. W. Stott, in his book entitled *Confess Your Sins*, cited this quotation from the head of a large British mental home: "I could dismiss half of my patients tomorrow if they could be assured of forgiveness" ([Waco, Tex.: Word, 1974], p. 73).

Forgiveness is man's deepest need now and in the future—for health and for heaven. Thus it is the first petition related to man's soul in the Disciples' Prayer. The first three petitions relate to God: "Hallowed be thy name," "thy kingdom come," "thy will be done in earth, as it is in heaven." The last three petitions relate to men: "Give us this day our daily bread," "forgive us our debts, as we forgive our debtors," "lead us not into temptation, but deliver us from evil." Of the three petitions related to men, the first speaks of physical sustenance, and the last two address spiritual sustenance. The order of the petitions is logical because we cannot live out spiritual principles unless we are alive physically.

The first request dealing with spiritual needs is for the forgiveness of sin, because that is man's deepest spiritual need. Before God can lead us or deliver us from temptation, we must have a relationship with Him, which is possible only when our sins are dealt with. God is "of purer eyes than to behold evil, and canst not look on iniquity" (Hab. 1:13). Isaiah 6:3 says, "Holy, holy, holy, is the Lord of hosts." There is no way that an absolutely holy God can be in the presence of unholy, sinful men. If we are to have a relationship with God, it will begin only with a petition for forgiveness. The word *forgive* appears six times in the Disciples' Prayer: twice in verse 12, two times in verse 14, and likewise in verse 15.

Review

We've learned that the Disciples' Prayer focuses primarily on God. Its intent is to glorify Him. The very nature of prayer is that we are acknowledging total dependence on God. We will have no daily bread, no forgiveness of sin, and no leading in our lives apart from Him. Therefore, His is the preeminence, the power, and the glory in the kingdom.

I. GOD'S PATERNITY (v. 9*a;* see pp. 22-31)

II. GOD'S PRIORITY (v. 9*b;* see pp. 36-49)

III. GOD'S PROGRAM (v. 10*a;* see pp. 59-69)

IV. GOD'S PLAN (v. 10*b;* see pp. 77-87, 94-107)

V. GOD'S PROVISION (v. 11; see pp. 115-24, 128-41)

Lesson

VI. GOD'S PARDON (vv. 12, 14-15)

"Forgive us our debts, as we forgive our debtors. . . . For if ye forgive men their trespasses, your heavenly Father will also forgive you; but if ye forgive not men their trespasses, neither will your Father forgive your trespasses."

According to Jesus' model of prayer, we are to routinely speak to God about the forgiveness of our sins.

Four Biblical Principles About Sin and Forgiveness

There are four principles about sin and forgiveness that I'd like to discuss before we begin our study of the text.

1. Sin makes man guilty and brings judgment

The principle that sin makes man guilty and brings judgment is a basic truth. Any of us who have been exposed to the teachings of God's Word know that to be true. Sin makes us guilty and calls for judgment. That's the human dilemma: Man is a sinner.

The Bible says that sin is lawlessness (1 John 3:4). It is the violation of God's standard. Romans 3:19 says that we are all guilty before God. We break His laws and are therefore guilty. Romans 6:23 says, "The wages of sin is death." Every man across the face of the earth stands in judgment before God on account of his sins.

2. Forgiveness is offered by God through Christ's death

God is a holy God, and every man and woman in society is sinful. But God is also a merciful, loving, and forgiving God, and He has offered forgiveness to man. Even though man is guilty and deserving of judgment, the Lord is willing to

148

forgive. The Bible says He will "remember [our] sin no more" (Jer. 31:34). He will pass by our iniquities and bury them in the depths of the sea (Mic. 7:18-19). Psalm 103:12 says, "As far as the east is from the west, so far hath he removed our transgressions from us." The prophets and apostles constantly wrote of God's forgiveness.

God wants to forgive us of our sins. However, He can't just overlook them; the penalty has to be paid somewhere. First Peter 2:24 tells us that Christ bore in His own body all the sins of every person who ever lived and paid the price of death for them. First John 2:2 says, "He is the propitiation for our sins, and not for ours only, but also for the sins of the whole world." According to 2 Corinthians 5:21, God "made him, who knew no sin, to be sin for us." Why? Because a just and holy God cannot forgive sin unless its penalty is paid. Christ paid that penalty, and forgiveness is offered by God on the basis of His death.

3. Confession of sin is necessary to receive forgiveness

Forgiveness is available from God. The penalty has been paid, and God is satisfied with it. Man only needs to receive that forgiveness by confessing his sins to God. Paul taught that "repentance toward God, and faith toward our Lord Jesus Christ" resulted in salvation (Acts 20:21). Thus, confession of sin is necessary. First John 1:9 says in effect, "Those who are confessing their sins are the ones giving evidence that they are being forgiven."

No man ever receives salvation unless he is repentant over his sinfulness. In the Beatitudes, our Lord was saying, "This is how a person enters My kingdom: First you must acknowledge that you are a beggar in spirit and that you are destitute and have no resources available to you in the midst of your sinfulness. You must mourn over your sin, be meek before God, and hunger and thirst for righteousness. When you plead for God's mercy, He will give it to you" (Matt. 5:3-7).

In Luke 18, we read of a Pharisee who entered the Temple and said, "God, I thank thee that I am not as other men are, extortioners, unjust, adulterers, or even as this tax collector. I fast twice in the week; I give tithes of all that I possess" (vv. 11-12). In contrast, we read in verse 13 of the tax collector, who "standing afar off, would not lift up so much as his eyes unto heaven, but smote upon his breast, saying, God be merciful to me a sinner." Jesus said, "I tell you, this man [the tax collector] went down to his house justified rather than the other" (v. 14). The Pharisee remained unforgiven because he didn't acknowledge his sinfulness. To receive forgiveness, one must confess his sins. And God is eager to forgive us. First John 1:9 says He is "faithful and just to forgive us our sins, and to cleanse us from all unrighteousness."

4. We must forgive one another to receive forgiveness ourselves

When people read Matthew 6:14-15, they sometimes misunderstand what is being said. They say, "These verses seem to say that I need to forgive others before God will forgive me. But how can a non-Christian forgive someone else? How can he do a righteous act before he has a righteous nature?" Such questions come from a misunderstanding of the concept in verses 14-15, and we will deal with that later in our study of this text.

From the four principles we have just talked about, I have chosen some key terms to assist us in our study of verses 12, 14, and 15. *Sin* makes us guilty, *forgiveness* is offered by God, *confession* is necessary, and *forgiving others* is essential. Those terms will help us to understand the text better.

A. The Problem—Sin

1. The width of sin

Matthew 6:12 uses the word *debts*, and verses 14-15 use the word *trespasses*. Both words refer to sin. The problem of every man is sin. Romans 3:10 says, "There is none righteous, *no, not one*" (emphasis added). The Lord inserted those last few words because He knew that if He didn't, someone would probably come along and say, "Except me." But God said no one is righteous. Verse 12 continues, "They are all gone out of the way, they are together become unprofitable [Gk., *achreioō*, "to go bad," as when milk becomes sour]; there is none that doeth good, no, not one." Verse 19 reads, "Now we know that whatever things the law saith, it saith to them who are under the law, that every mouth may be stopped, and all the world may become guilty before God." Then in verse 23 Paul writes, "All have sinned, and come short of the glory of God."

In Romans chapter 5 we read, "By one man [Adam] sin entered into the world, and death by sin, and so death passed upon all men, for all have sinned" (v. 12). That confirms everyone is a sinner. Sin disturbs every relationship in the human realm. It stirs up cosmic chaos. It waits to attack every baby born into the world. David said, "In sin did my mother conceive me" (Ps. 51:5). Iniquity begins from the moment a person is born.

Sin is the monarch that rules the heart of every man. It is the first lord of the soul, and its virus has contaminated every living being. Sin is the degenerative power in humanity that makes man susceptible to disease, illness, death, and hell. It is the culprit in every broken marriage, disrupted home, shattered friendship, argument, pain, sorrow, and death. No wonder Scripture says that sin is an accursed thing (Josh. 7:13). It is compared to the venom of snakes and the stench of death (Rom. 3:13).

2. The work of sin

Tragically, from the viewpoint of human resources, there is nothing that can be done about sin. Jeremiah 13:23 says, "Can the Ethiopian change his skin or the leopard its spots? Neither can you do good who are accustomed to doing evil" (NIV).

a) It dominates man's life

Man is hopeless; sin dominates his mind (Rom. 1:21). He has a reprobate mind given over to evil and lust. Sin also dominates the will. In Jeremiah 44:15-17 we read of men who wanted to do evil. Why? Because their will was controlled by sin. Our affections and emotions are also dominated by sin. John 3 says, "This is the condemnation, that light is come into the world, and men loved darkness rather than light" (v. 19).

b) It brings man under Satan's control

Ephesians 2:2 says that men are guided by "the prince of the power of the air, the spirit that now worketh in the sons of disobedience."

c) It brings man under God's wrath

According to Ephesians 2:3, unsaved people are "children of wrath." They are bull's-eyes for the guns of God's judgment.

d) It subjects man to misery

Man's life is made utterly miserable by sin. Job said, "Man is born unto trouble, as the sparks fly upward" (5:7). In Isaiah 57:21 we read, "There is no peace, saith my God, to the wicked." Romans 8:20 says, "The creation was made subject to vanity."

Man's whole life is color-stained with sin. There are more than fifty million people who die every year and face the ultimate consequence of sin. So man has a deep problem. When we pray, we are to deal with our sinfulness through confession.

3.   The words for sin

    a)   *Hamartia*

        The Greek word *hamartia* is probably used more than any other word in the New Testament in reference to sin. It means "to miss the mark." It was an archer's term: You shoot an arrow and it falls short of the target. That's why Romans 3:23 says all men have sinned and fallen short of the glory of God. No matter how far you shoot your arrow—no matter how good you try to be—you will never reach the mark. Some people may do better than others, but no one can reach the target. And what is the mark? Our Lord stated it earlier in the Sermon on the Mount, in Matthew 5:48: "Be ye, therefore, perfect, even as your Father, who is in heaven, is perfect." When you're as righteous as God, you hit the mark; but if you're not, you don't. However, we have all missed the mark.

    b)   *Parabasis*

        The Greek word *parabasis* is another word in the New Testament that is used to refer to sin. It basically means "to step across a line." God has drawn the line between right and wrong, and when we sin, we step across that line. It's like walking on a lawn with a sign posted nearby that says Keep Off the Grass. We see that warning, yet something in us makes us want to rebel. It is a part of our nature to do that. Sin, then, is stepping across the line between right and wrong. It is carrying out a forbidden thought, word, or deed.

    c)   *Anomia*

        Anomia is another Greek word used to speak of sin. It comes from the root word *nomos*, which means "law." *Anomia* conveys the idea of lawlessness. It refers to flagrantly breaking God's law.

There is a progression in the terms we've been looking at. *Hamartia*, the first word we discussed, has to do with missing the mark because of our incapacity to hit it. Our nature causes us to fall short. The second word, *parabasis*, refers to actually being compelled to sin. We can't restrain ourselves from doing something that is forbidden. But *anomia* speaks of open rebellion against God. It was used to refer to a man who kicks against the traces, who doesn't want God making any claim on his life. Rather, he does whatever he wants to. There is a soldier in British author Rudyard Kipling's *Mandalay* who says, "Ship me somewheres east of Suez, where the best is like the worst, where there aren't no Ten Commandments, an' a man can raise a thirst." That soldier didn't want anything to do with God's standards; he rebelled violently.

d) *Paraptōma*

The Greek word for "trespasses" in Matthew 6:14-15 is *paraptōma*. It means "to slip or fall." That's somewhat like the Greek word *hamartia* because it emphasizes our inability. There are times when we fall into sin. Galatians 6:1 says, "If a man be overtaken in a fault [*paraptōma*], ye who are spiritual restore such an one." It's hard to keep from sinning; we all do at one time or another. We get swept away by some temptation in the passion of the moment or because of loss of self-control.

e) *Opheilēma*

The word *debt* in Matthew 6:12 is translated from the Greek word *opheilēma*. Interestingly, it's used as a noun only twice in the New Testament—in Matthew 6:12 and Romans 4:4. Its verb form is used many times. Thus we are not very familiar with its precise meaning as a noun, but the verb form is used twenty-eight times to refer to a moral debt and seven times in reference to a monetary debt. Sin is a debt. When you sin, you owe to God a consequence or a debt because you have violated His holiness. It's like when a parent tells his children, "You do that, and you'll get one whack. You do it again, and you'll get two." If the children persist in doing wrong, they will have a debt to be paid. God keeps a record of your debt. At the Great White Throne Judgment, He will judge the ungodly from the books that record those debts (Rev. 20:12). How will they pay those debts? By spending eternity in hell.

Why Does Matthew Say "Debts" and Luke Say "Trespasses"?

Among the Jewish people in the New Testament era, the most common word used to speak of sin was *choba*, which is an Aramaic word. They spoke Aramaic in their everyday conversation, not the Greek the New Testament was written in. *Choba* means "debt." To a Jew, the primary responsibility in life was to obey God. When you disobeyed God, you owed Him a debt for your disobedience. So the Jews thought of sin as a debt.

Matthew used the word translated "debt" in his gospel, but when Luke recorded the Disciples' Prayer, he wrote, "Forgive us our sins [or 'trespasses']" (11:4). He was speaking in a more formal manner. Matthew, with his Jewish background, zeroed in on the concept of debt in his gospel because he knew that's the way the Jewish people viewed sin.

4. The wages of sin

Arthur W. Pink said, "As it is contrary to the holiness of God, sin is a defilement, a dishonour and reproach to us; as it is a violation of His law, it is a crime; and as to the guilt which we contact thereby, it is a debt. As creatures we owed a debt of obedience unto our Maker and Governor, and through failure to render the same on account of our rank disobedience we have incurred a debt of punishment, and it is for this latter that we implore the Divine pardon" (*An Exposition on the Sermon on the Mount* [Grand Rapids: Baker, 1974], pp. 163-64). That's true; as a result of our unrelenting sin, we owe such a massive debt to God that we can never pay it ourselves.

Our debt is like that of the unfaithful servant in Matthew 18, who owed so much he could have never paid the debt in his lifetime. That is our problem: We are sinners who owe a debt so monstrous it can't be paid. If you want to come to God, you must come to Him in recognition of that debt. Peter said, "Depart from me; for I am a sinful man, O Lord" (Luke 5:8). In 1 Timothy 1:15, Paul says he is the chief of sinners.

When Jesus taught us to pray "forgive us our debts" He verified the universality of the problem of sin. If we are to pray that, then we are to admit it's our problem. According to John 16:8, the Holy Spirit came into the world to convict it of sin. Any man who honestly faces the reality of his character cannot overlook his debt to God and the need to be forgiven.

B. The Provision—Forgiveness

If sin is the problem, forgiveness is the answer. Matthew 6:12 says "forgive us our debts." Forgiveness is available. Also, notice the word *us*. That points out the collective nature of the prayer. It encompasses all other believers, not just you. There is a sense of community in that verse. We are all in the same boat; we all need forgiveness.

1. The clarification about forgiveness

What is forgiveness? What does it mean for God to forgive you? Remember that according to the second principle we learned about sin on pages 146-47, forgiveness is available because of Christ's death.

Basically, forgiveness is God passing by our sin. It is God wiping our sin off the record. It is His setting us free from punishment and guilt. Micah 7:18-19 speaks of that: "Who is a God like unto thee, who pardoneth iniquity, and passeth by the transgression of the remnant of his heritage? He retaineth not his anger forever, because he delighteth in mercy. He will turn again; he will have compassion upon us; he will subdue our iniquities; and thou wilt cast all their sins into the depths of the sea." In Jeremiah 31:34 the Lord says, "I will remember their sin no more."

Simply stated, forgiveness is the removal of our sin, the covering of our sin, the blotting out of our sin, and the forgetting of our sin. According to Isaiah 53:6, God takes away our sin: "The Lord hath laid on him [Christ] the iniquity of us all." God has also covered our sin. Psalm 85:2 says, "Thou hast covered all their sin." In Isaiah 43:25 God tells us, "I, even I, am he who blotteth out thy transgressions." And last, He forgets our sin (Jer. 31:34). He literally eliminates any remembrance of our sin.

If you have reached a place in your Christian life where you view forgiveness as something ordinary, then you have lost your joy and come to a dry place in your life. We should be thankful to God for His forgiveness, which is possible only because of Christ. God couldn't just pass by your sin unless He executed just punishment, and that' why Christ died.

2. The categories of forgiveness

   There are two kinds of forgiveness: judicial forgivenes and parental forgiveness.

   a) Judicial forgiveness

      (1) The pronouncement

         Judicial forgiveness views God as a judge. God looks down and says, "You are guilty. You hav broken the law, and therefore you must be pur ished." But then He says, "Christ bore you punishment when He died on the cross. He too your guilt; He paid for your sin. The price is paid and I declare you to be forgiven." That is judicial act. God, as the moral judge of th universe, has granted us positional forgivenes By that act of judicial forgiveness, all your sins– past, present, and future—are completely fo given. You are justified forever. When does tha happen? The moment you place your faith i Jesus Christ and invite Him into your life. At tha moment, your sin is put on Him and His righ teousness is put on you (Rom. 3:24-26).

      (2) The payment

         When you receive Christ, God judicially declare you justified. Positionally now and forever, a your sins are covered, passed over, blotted ou and forgotten. And God continually cleanses u of sin, all because of what Christ did on the cros In Matthew 26:28 Jesus says, "This is my blood the new testament, which is shed for many fo the remission of sins." Paul writes in Ephesiar 1:7, "We have redemption through [Christ' blood, the forgiveness of sins." First John 2: reads, "Your sins are forgiven you for his name sake." Ephesians 4:32 says, "God, for Christ sake, hath forgiven you." Because Christ took our sins and paid the penalty, we are judicial declared righteous when we believe in Him ar accept His sacrifice. Past, present, and future si are all forgiven.

Were the Old Testament Saints Saved Through Christ?

Some people believe that judicial forgiveness applies only to New Testament saints and anyone since that time. They say that in the Old Testament, a person was saved until he sinned, and then he needed to offer another sacrifice to God to be saved again. However, salvation in the Old Testament is the same as it is in the New; it's based on trusting in and submitting to God.

Redemption in the Old Testament was just as instantaneous and sustained as in the New Testament. For example, James 2:23 says, "Abraham believed God." Abraham came to a point in his life when he had faith in God. He exercised that faith by believing all that God had revealed to him and accepting Him as his Lord and Savior. All that was done even though he had never seen the cross or perceived all that Christ would be. As a result of his belief, James 2:23 tells us, "It [Abraham's faith] was imputed unto him for righteousness; and he was called the friend of God." He was saved because of his faith in God.

Romans 4:3 says, "Abraham believed God, and it was counted unto him for righteousness." Later on we read, "To him that . . . believeth on him that justifieth the ungodly, his faith is counted for righteousness. . . . Blessed are they whose iniquities are forgiven, and whose sins are covered. Blessed is the man to whom the Lord will not impute sin" (vv. 5, 7-8). So from the moment Abraham believed, God never imputed sin to him again because his sins were placed on Christ.

Although the Old Testament saints lived prior to Christ's death, all their sins were put on Christ at the moment of their faith in the true God. Christ is the apex of history. Whether someone lived before or after Him, Christ still bore every man's sins. By an act of faith at a certain moment, the value of Christ's redemption is applied to those who believe God. Psalm 103:3 says God is the One who "forgiveth all thine iniquities, who healeth all thy diseases." I believe the Old Testament saints knew judicial redemption; their sins were nailed to the cross when they believed God.

Colossians 2:13-14 illustrates well what we're talking about. All through our lives, God keeps a record of our sins. As time goes along, our debt to God gets worse and worse. And we have no capacity to pay the debt at all. But look what happens as a result of Christ's death on the cross: "You, being dead in your sins and the uncircumcision of your flesh, hath he made alive together with him, having forgiven you all trespasses, blotting out the handwriting of ordinances that was against us, which was contrary to us, and took it out of the way, nailing it to his cross" (Col. 2:13-14). When a criminal was crucified, a list of all his crimes was nailed to the top of the cross so that the world could see why he was being crucified. When Jesus died on the cross, God pulled out of the record book the pages citing the sins of all those who would become believers and nailed them to the cross as if they were the crimes of Jesus. When Christ died, He paid the penalty for every crime that was nailed to His cross, and God blotted them out. That's judicial forgiveness.

What a joy it is to know that we are ultimately and forever forgiven in Christ! In Shakespeare's *Richard the III*, the evil king said, "My conscience hath a thousand several tongues, and every tongue brings in a several tale, and every tale condemns me" (Act V.iii.194). A Christian doesn't have to say the same thing. He can say with Paul, "Who is he that condemneth?" (Rom. 8:34). It is certainly not the God who justifies us (Rom. 8:33). If God, who occupies the highest court in the universe, declares you just, no one can condemn you. Nothing can separate you from the love of Christ (Rom. 8:35-39).

(3) The purification

In Hebrews 10 there is a comparison of the sacrificial system of Israel with the sacrifice of Christ. Verse 10 says, "We are sanctified through the offering of the body of Jesus Christ once for all." The word translated "sanctified" means "to be made pure, to be set apart." We are made holy by the one sacrifice of Christ. His death doesn't have to be repeated. When He died and we believed, His sacrifice was sufficient. He said on the cross, "It is finished" (John 19:30). The phrase "we are sanctified" in Hebrews 10:10 appears as a perfect participle with a finite verb in the Greek text. We see here the permanent, continuous state of salvation that issues from Christ's one sacrifice.

Verse 11 offers a contrast of the Old Testament priests who had stood "daily ministering and offering often the same sacrifices." Their job was never done. Then verse 12 says, "But [Christ], after he had offered one sacrifice for sins forever, sat down." Why? His work was finished. The priests offered sacrifices that had no lasting effect, but Christ offered one that had a permanent effect. It can't be repeated and doesn't need to be. Verse 14 says, "For by one offering he hath perfected forever them that are sanctified."

If Jesus says in Matthew 5:48 "be ye . . . perfect" and He made that perfection available through the cross, then He is the solution to the problem of sin. We are to be perfect, and He perfects us in His one offering. That is judicial forgiveness, the result of which is mentioned in Hebrews 10:17: "Their sins and iniquities will I remember no more." When you place your faith in Christ, all your sins will be forgiven.

Focusing on the Facts

1. What is the most essential, blessed, and difficult thing God ever did for man? Explain (see p. 146).
2. What twofold effect does sin have on man (see p. 146)?
3. What does the first petition in the Disciples' Prayer regarding man's spiritual need deal with? Why (see p. 147)?
4. What does the Bible say about sin? Support your answer with Scripture. What does man's sinfulness make him worthy of (see p. 148)?
5. What is God willing to do for us concerning our sinfulness? Can God simply overlook our sins? Explain your answer (see pp. 148-49).
6. According to Paul, what results in salvation (Acts 20:21; see p. 149)?
7. Discuss how a man enters God's kingdom, according to the Beatitudes (see p. 149).
8. Is sin the problem of *every* man? Support your answer with Scripture (see pp. 150-51).
9. What does Jeremiah 13:23 say about man's ability to change his sinful state (see p. 151)?
0. Describe the different ways sin affects us (see pp. 151-52).
1. What does the Greek word *hamartia* mean? How does it relate to man (see p. 152)?
2. Discuss the shades of meaning in the Greek words *parabasis* and *anomia* (see pp. 152-53).

13. The word *debt* in Matthew 6:12 is translated from the Greek word *opheilēma*. What concept is behind that word (see p. 153)?
14. As a result of our unrelenting _____, we _____ such a massive _____ to God that we can never pay it ourselves (see p. 154).
15. What is communicated by the word *us* in the petition in Matthew 6:12 (see p. 155)?
16. What is forgiveness (see pp. 155-56)?
17. What does Micah 7:18-19 tell us about God's forgiveness (see p. 155)?
18. When does a person become forgiven of his sins (see p. 156)?
19. What allowed forgiveness to become available to man? Support your answer with Scripture (see p. 156).
20. How were the Old Testament saints saved (see pp. 157-58)?
21. What is the point of the illustration in Colossians 2:13-14 (see p. 158)?
22. What result does Christ's one sacrifice have on our sins (Heb. 10:17; see pp. 158-59)?

Pondering the Principles

1. According to Romans 3:10-11, who is a sinner? What does 1 John 3:4 say about those who are sinners? Is there anything man can do to be spared of his sinful state (Titus 3:5)? How then can a person become saved (Eph. 2:8-9)? Is God willing to forgive anyone who comes to Him (Isa. 55:7; John 6:37)? Using what you have just learned, discuss how you would share with a non-Christian why sin is a terrible problem and what the solution is to that problem.

2. What is usually your first response when someone hurts you or wrongs you? Have there been times recently when you've held a grudge or sought revenge? Read the parable of the servant in Matthew 18:23-35. That servant owed the king an unpayable debt. According to verse 27, what did the king do in response to the servant's pleading in verse 26? What did that same servant do later on (vv. 28-30)? Do you find yourself more ready to receive forgiveness from God than to grant it to others? What command are we given in Matthew 18:21-22 regarding forgiveness? Determine the steps you need to take to develop a more forgiving heart.

3. God's willingness to forgive us in spite of our sinfulness should be a cause for rejoicing and thankfulness. Take some time now to write down why God's forgiveness of your sins is so important to you, and lift those thoughts to Him in gratitude.

10
The Pardon of Prayer—Part 2

Outline

Introduction

Review
I. God's Paternity (v. 9a)
II. God's Priority (v. 9b)
III. God's Program (v. 10a)
IV. God's Plan (v. 10b)
V. God's Provision (v. 11)
VI. God's Pardon (vv. 12, 14-15)
    A. The Problem—Sin ·
        1. The width of sin
        2. The work of sin
        3. The words for sin
        4. The wages of sin
    B. The Provision—Forgiveness
        1. The clarification about forgiveness
        2. The categories of forgiveness
           a) Judicial forgiveness
Lesson
           b) Parental forgiveness
               (1) Defined
               (2) Demonstrated
                  (a) Dealing with our daily sins
                     i) Psalm 51
                     ii) 1 John 1
                     iii) John 13
                  (b) Receiving God's daily forgiveness
    C. The Plea—Confession
        1. It is difficult
        2. It is desirable

Introduction

In the Disciples' Prayer are three petitions related to our needs. The first petition speaks of physical sustenance (v. 11), and the last two deal with our spiritual sustenance (vv. 12-13). In this lesson we will continue to look at verse 12, which says, "Forgive us our debts, as we forgive our debtors." That petition is footnoted later on in verses 14 and 15.

As we examine this important statement, we are endeavoring to understand the matter of dealing with sin in the Christian life. Even those who are believers still have a sin problem that must be faced. The petition in Matthew 6:12 is made by one who already belongs to God. The fact that the prayer begins "our Father" affirms that there is a living relationship with God through faith. Thus, as believers, we are to pray "forgive us our debts" after we have affirmed that God's name be hallowed, His kingdom come, His will be done, and that He sustains our physical needs. Then we are to acknowledge that we need the Lord's forgiveness. There are some people who think that once you are a Christian, you don't need to confess your sins or seek forgiveness, but that's not true. The Disciples' Prayer makes it clear that those who call God their Father must also ask for His forgiveness.

Review

I. GOD'S PATERNITY (v. 9*a;* see pp. 22-31)

II. GOD'S PRIORITY (v. 9*b;* see pp. 36-49)

III. GOD'S PROGRAM (v. 10*a;* see pp. 59-69)

IV. GOD'S PLAN (v. 10*b;* see pp. 77-87, 94-107)

V. GOD'S PROVISION (v. 11; see pp. 115-24, 128-41)

VI. GOD'S PARDON (vv. 12, 14-15)

As we learned from the last lesson, there are four key terms that can help us to better understand verse 12 and the footnote in verses 14-15: sin, forgiveness, confession, and forgiving others.

A. The Problem—Sin (see pp. 150-55)

The phrase "forgive us" in Matthew 6:12 implies that we have done something that requires forgiveness. The word "debt" in that same verse refers to sin, as does the word "trespasses" in verses 14-15. Sin is a reality in the life of a Christian. You don't suddenly stop sinning when you become a believer, nor do you lose your sensitivity to sin. In fact, you become more sensitive to it. As a Christian matures, the frequency of his sinning decreases, but his sensitivity to sin increases.

Sin makes us guilty and brings judgment. When there is sin in our lives, there is judgment. Hebrews 12:6 says, "[Those] whom the Lord loveth he chasteneth, and scourgeth every son whom he receiveth." Part of that chastening is in response to our sinfulness.

1. The width of sin (see pp. 150-51)

2. The work of sin (see p. 151-52)

3. The words for sin (see pp. 152-54)

   a) *Hamartia*—This means "to miss the mark." No one can attain perfection; everyone falls short of God's glory.

   b) *Parabasis*—This refers to stepping across a line. God draws a line and says, "Stay behind it," but we step across.

   c) *Anomia*—This means "lawlessness." We break God's laws.

   d) *Paraptōma*—This is the Greek word translated "trespasses" in Matthew 6:14-15. It means "to slip" or "to fall." We can't stay on the straight and narrow way.

   e) *Opheilēma*—This Greek word speaks of the concept of debt. Because our sins have violated God's holiness, we are in debt to Him. We have to deal with that debt by seeking His forgiveness.

4. The wages of sin (see pp. 154-55)

If we deny that we are sinners, that's the biggest problem of all, because if we say we have no sin, we make God out to be a liar (1 John 1:10).

B. The Provision—Forgiveness

The word *forgive* appears a total of six times in Matthew 6:12, 14-15; it appears twice in each of those verses. Forgiveness is offered by God on the grounds of Christ's death. Our sin problem can be dealt with by asking God for forgiveness. Therefore, we must recognize our sinfulness and seek His forgiveness. A Christian who says he doesn't sin is in a desperate situation because he is not seeking the solution he needs. There are some people who teach that Christians can reach a place in their lives where they no longer sin. But that's not true. Every Christian will continue to sin, and if he doesn't seek forgiveness, he will lose the meaningfulness of his relationship to God.

How is it possible that God can forgive us? And how does that forgiveness work? Forgiveness is possible because of Christ's death on the cross. God had to deal with our sins; a price had to be paid. Thus God took all the sins of the world and placed them on Christ, who took punishment for us by dying on the cross. On that basis, forgiveness is possible because the price has been paid.

1. The clarification about forgiveness (see pp. 155-56)

2. The categories of forgiveness

    a) Judicial forgiveness (see pp. 156-59)

    This is the complete positional forgiveness granted by God, the moral judge of the universe. Through it our past, present, and future sins are completely forgiven forever. We are justified and declared righteous for eternity the moment we put our faith in Jesus Christ. God drops the gavel of His sovereignty and says, "Declared righteous in Christ." That is an absolute, positional truth; it is eternal, as God is eternal. The moment you put your faith in Christ, God's righteousness is placed upon you. Thus the price for your sin is paid, and God is satisfied. That's why Romans 8:35 says, "What shall separate us from the love of Christ?" Verse 33 tells us that no one can ever lay any charge to God's elect.

    Now, if a Christian's sins are all forgiven and God has declared him righteous, why should he pray "forgive us our debts"? That is answered by considering the second category of forgiveness.

Lesson

    b) Parental forgiveness

    (1) Defined

    I use that title to refer to this aspect of forgiveness because the Disciples' Prayer begins with the phrase "our Father." Here, we are not dealing with God as a righteous judge but as a loving

Father. Just because we have been judicially forgiven doesn't mean we will stop sinning.

Although all our sins have been forgiven, each sin we commit affects our relationship with God. The relationship itself doesn't end, but the intimacy of it can be lost. For example, if one of my children sins against me by disobeying me, that doesn't mean I'm no longer his father. I remain his father, and there is a certain forgiveness in my heart already because he is in my family. But a sense of intimacy in my relationship with him is lost until he comes to me and says, "Daddy, I'm sorry." Then the intimacy is restored.

I'm happily married to my wife, and our relationship keeps getting better all the time. If I sin against my wife by a thoughtless deed or unkind word, that doesn't change our relationship. There is a sense in which I am automatically forgiven because I'm under the umbrella of her constant love. But some of the intimacy in our relationship will be lost until I ask her forgiveness.

That's the kind of forgiveness Christ is talking about in Matthew 6:12. He isn't talking about an unbeliever asking for forgiveness to become saved. Nor is He talking about a Christian who has to plead to God for forgiveness just because God doesn't want to forgive him. Recently on television someone asked a preacher this question: "If I die before I have a chance to confess a sin, will I still go to heaven?" The preacher said, "No; you'll go to hell." That is wrong, and it's terrible to instill that kind of fear into a believer. Every Christian has already been forgiven completely in salvation; Christ is talking about parental forgiveness in Matthew 6:12, forgiveness that gives us the fullness of joy in intimacy with God.

(2) Demonstrated

    (*a*) Dealing with our daily sins

        i) Psalm 51

           Psalm 51 illustrates parental forgiveness. King David, the author of the psalm, was redeemed. Righteousness had been imputed to his account because he believed, loved, and trusted in God. The righteousness of Christ, though yet future, has already been applied to him because of his faith.

During his lifetime, he committed two terrible sins: adultery and murder. Had he been anyone else but the king of Israel, he probably would have lost his life. Apparently he was considered to be above the law. Even though his sins were heinous, he was spared because of his position. But what I want you to notice is the nature of his prayer in Psalm 51, which came from his guilt- ridden, blood-stained heart as he reflected on his sin.

In verse 11 David says to God, "Cast me not away from thy presence, and take not thy holy Spirit from me." When he said that, he was referring to something he didn't want to have happen, not something that had already happened. God's presence and Spirit were still with David because he was redeemed. Even though David had committed adultery and murdered someone, he still knew the presence and Spirit of God because the Lord doesn't take back the gift of redemption. So David said, "Don't let the situation worsen more than it already has; don't take away your presence or Spirit." And God never will do that to any redeemed person.

Verse 14 reads, "Deliver me from bloodguiltiness, O God, thou God of my salvation." David affirmed his salvation in that verse. He cried out to a God whose presence and Spirit were still with him, and who would not take away his salvation. Yet even in affirming the judicial forgiveness of God, he sensed a loss of intimacy in his relationship with God.

That's why he cried out in verses 2-4, "Wash me thoroughly from mine iniquity, and cleanse me from my sin. For I acknowledge my transgressions, and my sin is ever before me. Against thee, thee only, have I sinned, and done this evil in thy sight." Then he said, "Purge me with hyssop, and I shall be clean; wash me, and I shall be whiter than snow."

There is a sense in which judicial forgiveness and parental forgiveness are different. David was saved (i.e., he had judicial forgiveness), but in Psalm 51 we notice a loss of intimacy in his relationship to God. Therefore he was asking for parental forgiveness. That's indicated in what David said next: "Make me hear joy and gladness, that the bones which thou hast broken may rejoice. . . . Create in me a clean heart, O God, and renew a right spirit within me. . . . Restore unto me the joy of thy salvation" (vv. 8, 10, 12). David wanted his joy back. He didn't say "restore my salvation"; he said "restore the joy of my salvation."

So judicial forgiveness takes care of salvation itself. Parental forgiveness deals with the joy of salvation. You can be saved and forgiven, but whenever you sin and don't confess it to God or deal with it right away, you forfeit the joy and fullness of your relationship with God.

ii) 1 John 1

In verse 3 John writes, "That which we have seen and heard declare we unto you, that ye also may have fellowship with us; and truly our fellowship is with the Father, and with His Son, Jesus Christ." He was saying, "We preach to bring you into the fellowship. We want to link you up with God, Christ, and those who are believers." That refers to judicial forgiveness; John preached so that people might have eternal life and be one in the fellowship.

John continues in verse 4, "And these things [i.e., everything written in 1 John] write we unto you, that your joy may be full." Thus, John preached the gospel message so that people would become a part of the fellowship. The contents of his epistle were written so that those in the fellowship would know full joy. Salvation brings you into the fellowship (an indication of judicial forgiveness), and obedience to the standards in God's Word lets you know the joy of that fellowship (an indication of parental forgiveness). In verse 9 John says that if you are in the fellowship, you'll be confessing your sins and God will be faithful to forgive your sins and cleanse you of all unrighteousness. Since confession of sin is discussed right after possessing full joy, we know that we will get full joy when we confess our sins. So the gospel brings judicial forgiveness, and obedience along with confession of sin will bring you the joy that comes from parental forgiveness.

iii) John 13

In this chapter, our dear Lord spoke of His love for the disciples in spite of their waywardness and sinfulness. At this time, they had been arguing about who would be the greatest in the kingdom. They were self-centered and indifferent toward Christ, unconcerned about His pending death. Their pride was ugly.

In the midst of the arguing, the Lord took off His outer garment, put a towel around His waist, and began to wash the disciples' feet (vv. 4-5). That was humiliating for both Christ and them. They should have washed His feet; He shouldn't have had to do that for them.

In verse 8, Jesus comes to Peter, who says, "Thou shalt never wash my feet." Peter wouldn't let the Lord stoop to doing that. Apparently Peter was facing his own sinfulness. He wouldn't allow Christ to wash his feet because he had just been arguing selfishly about who would be the greatest in the kingdom.

Jesus answered Peter, "If I wash thee not, thou hast no part with me" (v. 8). With that statement, the Lord turned the physical act of washing the disciples' feet into a tremendous spiritual truth. He was saying, "Peter, if you really want to know what it is to fellowship with Me and have a full relationship with Me, you had better let Me wash your feet." Then Peter said, "Lord, not my feet only, but also my hands and my head" (v. 9). Peter still didn't understand Jesus. The Lord responded, "He that is washed [i.e., bathed] needeth not except to wash his feet, but is entirely clean" (v. 10). Peter was already clean; Jesus wanted only to wash his feet. Peter first told Jesus what not to do, then he told Him what to do. Peter didn't understand the spiritual truth Christ was trying to teach.

In verse 10, Christ tells the disciples they were all clean, excepting one—they were all redeemed except for Judas. They had already been made righteous by faith. They didn't need an entire bath again. How many times does God make a person righteous? Once. All Christ needs to do is wash the dirt off our feet now and then. In those days, a person bathed his entire body in the morning. Then during the day, because everyone wore open sandals, his feet would get dirty as a result of the mud and dust on the roads. So whenever you entered into a home or a business to talk or to eat a meal, it was necessary to wash your feet as a matter of obvious propriety.

So Christ was telling the disciples, "You have already had judicial forgiveness. You had your spiritual bath when you became believers. All that's necessary for Me to do is keep the fullness of our relationship open by washing your feet." That speaks of parental forgiveness. As we walk through the world we collect its dust, which represents the sins we commit. And as we confess those sins, we are washed clean. As we continually confess our sins, God is faithful and just to keep on forgiving and cleansing us (1 John 1:9). Once you've been bathed in the saving blood of Jesus Christ, you've received judicial forgiveness and will never need it again. But parental forgiveness continues every day as we keep open the fullness of communion with God. Positional (judicial) purging needs no repetition, but practical (parental) purging has to be repeated every day.

Keeping the Joy in Your Relationship with God

When we pray, we need to pray in accord with Matthew 6. After we have acknowledged that God's name is to be hallowed, asked that His kingdom come and His will be done, and acknowledged that He is the source of our daily sustenance, we need to face the fact that our feet are dirty. We need to recognize that as long as we have unconfessed sins in our lives, there will be a loss of joy and intimacy in our communion with God. Every believer needs to open his heart daily for the forgiveness that keeps his life clean.

We see this principle exemplified in David's life. After David had confessed his terrible sin concerning Bathsheba and her husband, Uriah, the prophet Nathan told him, "The Lord also hath put away thy sin" (2 Sam. 12:13). David already had judicial forgiveness, but he still needed to confess his sin. You may know people who say, "The Lord has already forgiven all my sins; I don't need to worry about continually confessing them." But David didn't say that. Not long after Nathan confronts David in 2 Samuel 12:13, David writes Psalm 32, where he says to God, "I acknowledged my sin unto thee, and mine iniquity have I not hidden. I said, I will confess my transgressions unto the Lord" (v. 5). Even though David knew he already had judicial forgiveness, he cried out in confession for parental forgiveness to keep the intimacy of his relationship with God.

What are we to learn from the petition "forgive us our debts"? It is simply a plea for God to cleanse us moment by moment as we acknowledge our sins to Him. Confession is a necessary element in every believer's life.

(b) Receiving God's daily forgiveness

It thrills me to know that God is so eager to forgive. Most pagan religions view their gods as being like men. If you plead to them too much, they'll get sick of hearing you and say, "This is the last time I'm listening to you. From here on, you'll have to suffer the consequences of your sins. I've given you more forgiveness than ten people deserve." But God is not that way. Nehemiah said, "Thou are a God ready to pardon" (9:17). Micah wrote, "He delighteth in mercy" (7:18).

You might say, "But I keep having the same problem again and again and keep asking God for forgiveness. Doesn't He get sick of that?" No, because He delights in mercy. That's an act of His nature that gives Him glory. That's why Romans 5:20 says, "Where sin abounded, grace did much more abound." God loves to forgive. There is no way you can diminish His resource of forgiveness. He will forgive you as often as you come before Him in confession.

Someone once said to me, "A sermon you preached about judicial forgiveness ruined my son. He thought that because a believer's sins are covered for eternity at the moment of salvation, it was all right for him to go out and sin." I question whether that person's son even knew Christ, because if we know that God has forgiven all our sins and is eager to forgive us each time we confess our sins, that should deter us from sinning. We shouldn't abuse God's loving forgiveness by letting sin be present in our lives.

171

How Does Your Ability to Forgive Rate?

Theologian Donald Barnhouse, in a conversation with a college professor, told this story that illustrates what we're talking about: "A man had lived a life of great sin but had been converted and eventually had come to marry a fine Christian woman. He had confided to her the nature of his past life in a few words. As he had told her these things, the wife had taken his head in her hands and had drawn him to her shoulder and had kissed him, saying, 'John, I want you to understand something very plainly. I know my Bible well, and therefore I know the subtlety of sin, and the devices of Satan working in the human heart. I know you are a thoroughly converted man, John, but I know that you still have an old nature, and that you are not yet as fully instructed in the ways of God as you soon will be. The Devil will do all he can to wreck your Christian life, and he will see to it that temptations of every kind will be put in your way. The day might come—please God that it never shall—when you will succumb to temptation and fall into sin. Immediately the Devil will tell you that it is no use trying, that you might as well continue on in the way of sin, and that above all you are not to tell me because it will hurt me. But John, I want you to know that here in my arms is your home. When I married you I married your old nature as well as your new nature, and I want you to know there is full pardon and forgiveness in advance for any evil that may ever come into your life.'"

Dr. Barnhouse said that when he finished the story, the college professor lifted up his eyes reverently and said, "My God! if anything could ever keep a man straight that [kind of forgiving love] would be it!" (*God's Methods for Holy Living* [Grand Rapids: Eerdmans, 1951], pp. 72-74). That is exactly the nature of God's relationship with us.

C. The Plea—Confession

We receive God's forgiveness by confessing our sin. Matthew 6:12 speaks of confession. You can know about sin and forgiveness, but if you don't confess your sin, you won't receive forgiveness. As long as you harbor your sin and don't repent of it, you will not be free to know the joy God wants you to know. Sin creates a barrier that shatters the intimacy of fellowship. So we must confess our sin.

1. It is difficult

    It's hard to confess our sins at times. It's hard to get a child to admit he did something wrong. I remember that as a little boy I vandalized a school with another boy. My father was holding a revival meeting in a small town in Indiana. During that week, the other boy and I went to the school and vandalized it. Some people went from house to house in that town to find out who did it. They came to the house we were staying at, and my father and the owner of the house answered the door. A person asked, "Would your children happen to know about the vandalism that occurred at the school?" I held my father's hand and put on my most angelic face, doing everything I could to show that I was as spiritual as my evangelist father. My father patted me on the head and said, "Not Johnny. He's a wonderful boy." The other father said the same thing about his son.

    That night my father spoke at the tent meeting, and I went forward when he gave the invitation. I prayed with him and said, "I think I need Jesus in my heart," but he never knew why I did that. It wasn't until ten years later that I told him what I had done at the school. For ten years, I didn't have the courage to admit my wrongdoing. However, I'm not alone. Adam and Eve enjoyed great fellowship with God, but the minute they sinned, they hid from God (Gen. 3:8).

    As long as you don't confess your sins, you will forfeit your joy. Proverbs 28:13 says, "He that covereth his sins shall not prosper, but whoso confesseth and forsaketh them shall have mercy." Your spiritual prosperity is at stake when you hide your sins. That's why you need to say "forgive us our debts."

2. It is desirable

    Confession of sin is vital. David said to Nathan, "I have sinned against the Lord" (2 Sam. 12:13). Again in 2 Samuel 24:10 he says, "I have sinned greatly in what I have done . . . I have done very foolishly." In 1 Chronicles 21:17 he says, "I it is who has sinned and done evil indeed." The prophet Isaiah said, "I am a man of unclean lips, and I dwell in the midst of a people of unclean lips" (Isa. 6:5). Daniel confessed his sins to the Lord in prayer (Dan. 9:20). Peter says in Luke 5:8, "Depart from me; for I am a sinful man, O Lord." Paul said, "This is a faithful saying, and worthy of all acceptance, that Christ Jesus came into the world to save sinners, of whom I am chief" (1 Tim. 1:15).

Confessing sin isn't easy, but it's necessary so that we can experience the joy that comes with parental forgiveness. Don't conceal your sin. John Stott said, "One of the surest antidotes to this process of moral hardening is the disciplined practice of uncovering our sins of thought and outlook, as well as word and deed, and the repentant forsaking of them" (*Confess Your Sins* [Waco, Tex.: Word, 1974], p. 19). If you don't confess your sins, you will become hardened. I've seen Christians—judicially forgiven and eternally secure—who are hardened, impenitent, and insensitive to sin. Consequently, they are also without joy. They don't know the meaning of a loving intimate fellowship with God. They block it out with the barricade of their unconfessed sin.

A Look Inside a Repentant Heart

Let me relate some words from *The Valley of Vision: A Collection of Puritan Prayers and Devotions* (Carlisle, Pa.: Banner of Truth Trust], p. 76):

O God of grace,
Thou hast imputed my sin to my substitute,
   and hast imputed his righteousness to my soul,
      clothing me with a bridegroom's robe,
      decking me with jewels of holiness.
But in my Christian walk I am still in rags;
   my best prayers are stained with sin;
   my penitential tears are so much impurity;
   my confessions of wrong are so many aggravations of
      sin;
   my receiving the Spirit is tinctured with selfishness.

I need to repent of my repentance;
I need my tears to be washed;
I have no robe to bring to cover my sins,
   no loom to weave my own righteousness;
I am always standing clothed in filthy garments,
   and by grace am always receiving change of raiment,
   for thou dost always justify the ungodly;
I am always going into the far country,
   and always returning home as a prodigal,
   always saying, Father, forgive me,
   and thou art always bringing forth the best robe.

Every morning let me wear it,
    every evening return in it,
    go out to the day's work in it,
    be married in it,
    be wound to death in it,
    stand before the great white throne in it,
    enter heaven in it shining as the sun.
Grant me never to lose sight of
    the exceeding sinfulness of sin,
    the exceeding righteousness of salvation,
    the exceeding glory of Christ,
    the exceeding beauty of holiness,
    the exceeding wonder of grace.

Another prayer from the same book (p. 83) reads:

I am guilty but pardoned,
    lost, but saved,
    wandering, but found,
    sinning, but cleansed.
Give me perpetual broken-heartedness,
Keep me always clinging to thy cross,
Flood me every moment with descending grace,
Open to me the springs of divine knowledge,
    sparkling like crystal,
    flowing clear and unsullied
    through my wilderness of life.

Confession—the purging of the soul. That's the plea of the petition in Matthew 6:12. Is it part of your prayer life?

Focusing on the Facts

1. Are Christians sensitive to sin? Explain (see p. 163).
2. What do we do if we deny we are sinners (1 John 1:10; see p. 163)?
3. In considering parental forgiveness, we are dealing with God not as a righteous judge but as a ＿＿＿＿＿ ＿＿＿＿＿ (see pp. 164-65).
4. How does sin affect our relationship with God (see p. 165)?
5. How is parental forgiveness illustrated in Psalm 51 (see pp. 165-67)?
6. Judicial forgiveness takes care of ＿＿＿＿＿ itself. Parental forgiveness deals with the ＿＿＿＿＿ of ＿＿＿＿＿ (see p. 167).
7. What did John mean when he said, "These things we write unto you, that your joy may be full" (1 John 1:4; see p. 168)?
8. Discuss the distinction between judicial and parental forgiveness as Christ presented it in John 13 (see pp. 169-70).

9. What did David do in Psalm 32 even after he knew he had permanent, judicial forgiveness? Why (see pp. 170-71)?
10. How does God feel about forgiving people? Support your answer with Scripture (see p. 171).
11. What should a person's attitude be toward sin after God has granted him judicial forgiveness (see p. 171)?
12. What must we do to receive God's forgiveness (see p. 172)?
13. What does Proverbs 28:13 have to say about confession of sin (see p. 173)?
14. Give examples of people in the Bible who confessed their sins (see pp. 173-74).
15. What can happen to you if you don't confess your sins (see p. 174)?

Pondering the Principles

1. Read Matthew 4:1-11. What did Christ do to resist the temptation to sin? Are you currently using that approach to overcome temptation in your own life? Write down some of the temptations you frequently encounter. What are some appropriate Scripture passages that tell you the proper ways to respond to those temptations? Why would handling temptation in that manner be successful?

2. Do you have a habit of examining your life to make sure you have confessed any impurity within you? Read Job 31:6 and Psalm 119:11; 139:23-24. According to Scripture, what attitude should we have toward God in relation to our sins? Read Psalm 1. What kind of man is blessed (vv. 1-2)? What will such a man be like (v. 3)? When you confess your sins daily to the Lord, your relationship with Him will be filled with joy.

11
The Pardon of Prayer—Part 3

Outline

Introduction
A. The Joy of Forgiveness
B. The Need for Forgiveness
   1. From God
   2. For each other
      a) It is characteristic of the saints
      b) It follows the example of Christ
      c) It expresses the highest virtue of man
      d) It frees the conscience from guilt
      e) It delivers us from chastening

Review
  I. God's Paternity (v. 9*a*)
 II. God's Priority (v. 9*b*)
III. God's Program (v. 10*a*)
IV. God's Plan (v. 10*b*)
 V. God's Provision (v. 11)
VI. God's Pardon (vv. 12, 14-15)
   A. The Problem—Sin
   B. The Provision—Forgiveness
      1. The clarification about forgiveness
      2. The categories of forgiveness
         a) Judicial forgiveness
         b) Parental forgiveness
            (1) Defined
            (2) Demonstrated
   C. The Plea—Confession

Lesson
   D. The Prerequisite—Forgiving Others
      1. The interpretation
      2. The illustration

3. The implementation
   a) Removing grudges
      (1) Take your grudge to God as a sin
      (2) Go to the person in question
      (3) Give the person something you highly value
   b) Reviewing Scripture
      (1) Matthew 5:7
      (2) Matthew 5:21-25
      (3) Psalm 23:6
      (4) Psalm 66:18
      (5) James 2:13
      (6) Matthew 18

Introduction

A. The Joy of Forgiveness

Matthew 6:12 says, "Forgive us our debts, as we forgive our debtors." The word *forgive* strikes us immediately. *Forgiveness* may be the most wonderful word in any language. There is nothing better than knowing that your sins are all forgiven by God. It's reassuring to know that you have been forgiven by someone you grossly wronged or injured.

There is an unusual epitaph on a large headstone in a cemetery outside of New York City. The name of the person in the grave is not on the headstone. There is no mention of when the person was born or when he died. It doesn't say anything about being a beloved mother, father, husband, wife, brother, sister, son, or daughter. Just one word stretches across the headstone: *Forgiven.*

Someone wanted to show that he died in peace because he was forgiven.

Henry Ward Beecher, a nineteenth-century American preacher, said, "Let me saw off a branch from one of the trees that is now budding in my garden, and all summer long there will be an ugly scar where the gash has been made; but by next autumn it will be perfectly covered over by the growing; and by the following autumn it will be hidden out of sight; and in four or five years there will be but a slight scar to show where it has been; and in ten or twenty years you would never suspect that there had been an amputation. Trees know how to overgrow their injuries, and hide them: and love does not wait so long as trees do" (*Encyclopedia of 2585 Illustration* [Grand Rapids: Zondervan, n.d.], p. 260). Peter said that love covers a multitude of sins (1 Pet. 4:8). One who loves other is in a much bigger hurry to forgive than trees are. Forgiveness is a vital by-product of love.

B. The Need for Forgiveness

1. From God

God has said much in Scripture about forgiveness. It is man's deepest spiritual need. Apart from forgiveness, man cannot enter into a relationship with God, and he will pay the penalty for his sin and spend eternity in hell. Man must have forgiveness if he wants to know God and enjoy heaven. It is also the only way man can be delivered from the anxiety and guilt that sin brings to bear upon his life. Our need for forgiveness is the first of the two petitions concerning spiritual necessities in the Disciples' Prayer. It touches man at the deepest point of his need. Coming to God for forgiveness is the most vital requirement for any man.

There are some questions we all need to ask ourselves concerning forgiveness: Have you experienced the forgiveness that comes through trusting in Christ? If you have and you are a Christian, are you bringing your sins to the Lord on a day-to-day basis so that He can wash the dust of the world off your feet? Are you experiencing the joy and intimacy with God that comes from daily confession? How about forgiving others? Are you freeing others from the bondage of an offense by wholeheartedly forgiving them?

2. For each other

Forgiveness is a blessed virtue. In the last two lessons we have discussed God's forgiveness toward us; now I'd like for us to focus on our forgiveness toward others. Matthew 6:12 ends with the phrase "as we forgive our debtors." Then verses 14-15 say that if we forgive others, we will be forgiven; but if we don't forgive others, we won't be forgiven. It's important for us to forgive one another for several reasons.

a) It is characteristic of the saints

Christians are characterized as those who forgive. In Matthew 5:43 the Jewish rabbinical tradition taught, "Thou shalt love thy neighbor, and hate thine enemy." But the Lord said, "Love your enemies, bless them that curse you, do good to them that hate you, and pray for them who despitefully use you, and persecute you, that [you might manifest yourselves as] sons of your Father" (Matt. 5:44-45). Blessing those who persecute you is tantamount to forgiveness. By loving your enemies, you manifest that you are a son of God.

It is characteristic of the saints to forgive; after all, we have been forgiven. Have we so soon forgotten how God has forgiven us that we would not forgive someone else? When a Christian fails to forgive someone else, he sets himself up as a higher judge than God. The Lord's forgiveness is infinite, and it's impertinent for us to usurp His place as Judge.

b) It follows the example of Christ

First John 2:6 tells us that if we say we abide in Christ, we ought to walk as He walked. How did He walk? In forgiveness. Ephesians 4:32 says we are to forgive one another "even as God, for Christ's sake, hath forgiven you." Through Christ's death God has forgiven us for the sake of Christ, who is our pattern for forgiveness. In behalf of those who drove the nails through His hands, spit upon His face, mocked Him, and crushed a crown of thorns on His head, Jesus said, "Father, forgive them" (Luke 23:34). He is our role model. The severity of any offense toward us cannot match what Christ endured. The writer of Hebrews said, "You have not yet resisted to the point of shedding blood in your striving against sin" (12:4, NASB). None of us have endured what Christ endured. He forgave us and set the pattern for us to forgive one another.

c) It expresses the highest virtue of man

I believe a man most displays the majesty of his creation in the image of God when he expresses forgiveness. Proverbs 19:11 says, "The discretion of a man deferreth his anger, and it is his glory to pass over a transgression." The highest act of virtue a man can display is to overlook a transgression.

d) It frees the conscience from guilt

When there is a need to be forgiven and to forgive others, guilt is present. David, before he confessed his sinfulness in Psalm 32, faced several problems. Verse 4 says, "My moisture is turned into the

180

drought of summer." His body fluids—his lymphatic system, circulatory system, and saliva glands—were not working right. He was sick. In verse 3 he says, "My bones became old through my roaring all the day long." According to 2 Corinthians 2:10-11, when we have an unforgiving heart, we give Satan an advantage over us. We are to forgive one another to free our consciences of guilt.

A Warning About Grudges

People who carry grudges and have a bitter attitude toward others wound themselves. There is a chapter in S. I. McMillen's book *None of These Diseases* (Old Tappan, N. J.: Revell, 1984) that's entitled "It's Not What You Eat—It's What Eats You." It reflects an important truth. The following illustrations are from McMillen's book (pp. 111-12):

Dale Carnegie told this story about a grizzly bear in Yellowstone National Park. Some garbage was piled in a clearing, and the bear came to eat the garbage. Now the grizzly bear is probably the most ferocious animal on the North American continent; the only animal that could stand off a grizzly might be a Kodiak bear. So the grizzly doesn't have many enemies. While the bear was eating, a little skunk came to the clearing. He went to where the bear was and began eating. The skunk was very impudent, but the bear didn't do anything. They shared the food. Why? Because the bear knew the high cost of getting even. He didn't want to pay the price. He was smarter than many people who get goiters, heart attacks, and colitis as a result of holding a grudge.

A father went into a doctor's office one day with his fourteen-year-old son, and said to the doctor, "I only came to get some more pills for my wife's colitis." The boy immediately said, "Who was Ma colliding with this time?"

  e) It delivers us from chastening

Where there is an unforgiving spirit there is sin. And where there is sin, there is chastening. Hebrews 12:6 says, "Whom the Lord loveth he chasteneth, and scourgeth every son whom he receiveth." In 1 Corinthians 11, Paul rebukes the Corinthians for the animosity and bitterness they displayed at their love feasts. As a result of their vile behavior, many of them became sick, and some of them even died (v. 30). They lacked a proper love relationship to one another.

Those are reasons that forgiveness is important. Yet another reason, which we will examine in this lesson, is that if we don't forgive others, we won't be forgiven.

Review

I. GOD'S PATERNITY (v. 9*a*; see pp. 22-31)

II. GOD'S PRIORITY (v. 9*b*; see pp. 36-49)

III. GOD'S PROGRAM (v. 10*a*; see pp. 59-69)

IV. GOD'S PLAN (v. 10*b*; see pp. 77-87, 94-107)

V. GOD'S PROVISION (v. 11; see pp. 115-24, 128-41)

VI. GOD'S PARDON (vv. 12, 14-15)

In the Disciples' Prayer, Matthew 6:12 is the first petition regarding man's spiritual need. The first three petitions are concerned with God: "Hallowed be thy name," "thy kingdom come," "thy will be done" (vv. 9-10). Before you can pray for yourself, you have to give God His rightful place in your prayers. By the time you have gone through the first three petitions, you will have sidestepped your selfish desires and have the right perspective of yourself. We are also to acknowledge that it's God who provides our daily bread (v. 11). We wouldn't have a spiritual life if we weren't alive. God takes care of our physical needs. Then verse 12, which is the first petition concerning our spiritual needs, tells us that we need to deal with our sins. So, first we are to acknowledge God, then we are to pray for our physical and spiritual needs.

A. The Problem—Sin (see pp. 150-55)

B. The Provision—Forgiveness (see pp. 155-59, 163-72)

    1. The clarification about forgiveness (see pp. 155-56)

    2. The categories of forgiveness (see pp. 156-59)

        a) Judicial forgiveness (see pp. 156-59)

        This is the forgiveness that God grants to an unredeemed individual at the moment he puts his faith in Christ. God imputes to him the righteousness of Christ and declares him eternally righteous, forgiven, and justified.

b) Parental forgiveness (see pp. 164-72)

Some people ask, "If I'm judicially forgiven and every sin—past, present, and future—is covered by the blood of Christ, then why do I need to pray 'forgive us our debts'"? Such people think that the Disciples' Prayer is the prayer of an unbeliever. But what are the first two words in the prayer? "Our Father" (Matt. 6:9). You have to be in the family of God to say that. Then the question is posed, "If I am a believer and I already have judicial forgiveness as a result of my salvation, why do I need to ask for forgiveness?" The petition "forgive us our debts" refers to what I call parental forgiveness, which has to do with the joy of salvation, not the fact of it.

(1) Defined (see pp. 164-65)

(2) Demonstrated (see pp. 165-72)

Parental forgiveness is illustrated in John 13:10, where Jesus essentially said to Peter, "You have already been bathed; you don't need another bath. All you need is for your feet to be cleaned daily." When a person becomes saved, God bathes him in the righteousness of Christ. Thereafter, all the Lord wants to do is dust off the dirt that we get on our feet as we walk through the world. Judicial forgiveness is positional; it deals with our state before God. Parental forgiveness is practical and deals with our living in the world.

Parental forgiveness is also discussed in 1 John. There, the apostle John wrote, "Our fellowship is with the Father, and with his Son, Jesus Christ. And these things write we unto you, that your joy may be full" (1:3-4). Joy and productivity in our spiritual welfare are the issues there. After a believer becomes judicially saved, he doesn't become insensitive to sin or ignore it. Rather, he keeps on confessing it (1 John 1:9). Confession is a way of life. After we enter into salvation by faith, do we stop expressing faith thereafter? No, because "we walk by faith" (2 Cor. 5:7). We enter into salvation by confessing our sin, and that practice should never stop. It's to be a way of life.

First John 2 says that if we love God and are therefore true believers, we will love our Christian brothers (vv. 9-11). In addition, the obedience expressed at the moment of salvation will continue in our lives. Likewise, 1 John 1:9 says that if you are truly a believer, you will continue to confess your sin because your sensitivity to it grows from the time you were saved. Prior to salvation, you walked in darkness. But as a Christian, you walk in the light, and your sins stand out in contrast to the light. So John was talking about the daily cleansing that we need, not for salvation but for maintaining the intimacy of our fellowship with God. If my child sins against me, that doesn't mean I'm going to throw him out of the family. But he will have to make things right so that the intimacy of family fellowship can be restored.

So the petition in Matthew 6:12 requires a confession of sins to God. If you don't do that, you will short-circuit your spiritual effectiveness.

C. The Plea—Confession (see pp. 172-75)

The Greek word translated "confess" in 1 John 1:9 (*homologeō*) means "to say the same thing." To confess your sin is to agree with God about your sin and repent of it. Confession also includes thanking God for His forgiveness. Anything less than that is not true confession. We are to say, "Lord, I agree with what you say about my sin." As soon as you say that, you free God to chasten you without impunity because you admitted that you deserved it. If a person doesn't admit his sinfulness and God chastens him, the person often blames God for chastening without justification. That's why Joshua said to Achan, "My son, give, I pray thee, glory to the Lord God of Israel, and make confession unto him" (7:19). In other words, "God is going to judge you. You might as well admit you deserve that judgment before it takes place so God will be glorified." When you acknowledge your sin, you glorify God by recognizing His right to chasten you. Then you are to repent of your sin and thank God for His forgiveness.

First John 1:9 says that believers are continually confessing their sins and continually being forgiven. The words are in the present tense; confession is to be a way of life. Yet I find that many Christians don't confess their sins as they should

184

Every once in a while when they are desperate for help from God, they will. Some Christians ask God to forgive them in a general way. But we are to deal with our sins straightforwardly. When you do, you will know the fullness of blessing in your life. Every time you articulate your sin to the Lord in a specific manner, it becomes more difficult to return to that sin again. That's why some people aren't specific when they confess their sins because they don't want to give up a particular sin they enjoy.

Lesson

D. The Prerequisite—Forgiving Others

1. The interpretation

   Matthew 6:14-15 elucidates the phrase "as we forgive our debtors" at the end of verse 12. The literal rending of the aorist tense in the Greek text would make that phrase read "as we forgave our debtors." Thus the verse could read, "Forgive us our debts, as we have forgiven others." The idea is that before we ever seek forgiveness for our sins against God, we are to have already forgiven those who have sinned against us. (That's another indication that the Disciples' Prayer is not a prayer for unbelievers, because a non-Christian has no capacity to forgive others and thus be forgiven.) So the message to Christians is this: Before we ask the Lord to wash our feet each day, we have to make sure we have forgiven others. That's the prerequisite.

2. The illustration

   A person might say, "I go to church all the time. I read the Bible, listen to tapes, and go to seminars. But I don't have the joy I ought to have. I miss out on being used by God. I feel as if my life isn't all that it could be. I get tired of trying to get up to a certain spiritual standard." Someone might say that person needs to pray more, take a class on spiritual growth, read the Bible more, or read a specific book. Some people attempt to search for the joy they are supposed to be having without thinking about one possibility: Maybe they aren't confessing their sins. Perhaps they aren't going to the Lord and saying, "I admit that I am a sinner. Here are the sins; purify me." Some people will respond, "I'm already doing that and still don't have joy." I know some people who keep a list of their sins to confess them. Yet they still don't have fulfillment. Why? Confession of sin to the Lord isn't all that's necessary; they need to make sure they have forgiven others. By not forgiving others, you short-circuit your spiritual welfare.

These aren't my words; they are the Lord's words. He says we are to forgive others. So if you lack joy, examine your life at that level. J. Oswald Sanders said, "Jesus is here stating a principle in God's dealing with His children. He deals with us as we deal with others. He measures us by the yardstick we use on others. The prayer is not 'Forgive us *because* we forgive others,' but 'Forgive us *even* as we have forgiven others.'"

There are similar principles elsewhere in Scripture. Luke 6:38 says, "Give, and it shall be given unto you. . . . For with the same measure that ye measure it shall be measured to you again." Second Corinthians 9:6 says, "He who soweth sparingly shall reap also sparingly; and he who soweth bountifully shall reap also bountifully." God deals with us the way we deal with Him. We receive a return on whatever we invest in His kingdom. The same thing is true about confessing your sins and seeking forgiveness. God will deal with you the way you deal with others.

If you aren't experiencing full joy now, it may be because you are holding a grudge against someone. The Jewish people recognized that; one Jewish man who lived around 200 B.C. said that men must forgive if they want to be forgiven. The Talmud, the rabbinical commentary on the Old Testament, says that he who is indulgent toward other's faults will be mercifully dealt with by the supreme Judge (*Shabbath* 151*b*).

3. The implementation

   a) Removing grudges

      Are you forgiving? If you're not, God won't forgive you, and you will be going through the world with muddy feet. You will have judicial forgiveness and the righteousness of Christ imputed to you, but the joy and intimacy in your relationship with God will be missing. You won't be of any use to God.

      How are we to deal with our grudge? Here are three practical steps to removing a grudge.

186

(1) Take your grudge to God as a sin

When we feel bitter toward someone, we should pray, "Lord, this is the way I feel toward so-and-so. I acknowledge my sin and am sorry about it. I want to repent of it."

(2) Go to the person in question

This may be hard to do, but it's necessary if you want to know spiritual joy. You must decide if you want to forfeit joy to harbor your grudge. Otherwise, go to the person and say, "I need your forgiveness." The person you had a grudge against may have already forgiven you, and he may not even have known that he offended you.

(3) Give the person something you highly value

Giving the person something you value highly is a practical approach; let me explain why. Jesus said, "Where your treasure is, there will your heart be also" (Matt. 6:21). When you give someone something that is of value to you, your heart will go with it and that will change the way you feel toward that person. There have been times in my life when I felt bitter toward someone who wronged me, and I've applied that principle by giving the person a book or some other gift. I noticed that the moment I gave the gift I felt liberty in my spirit. There is no joy like the joy of giving. You will sense the same joy when you forgive others. You might try to confess your sins to the Lord without forgiving others, but you won't sense the freedom of forgiveness that way.

b) Reviewing Scripture

(1) Matthew 5:7

Jesus said, "Blessed are the merciful; for they shall obtain mercy." If you want to receive mercy from God, then you must be merciful. That's a principle of spiritual life. People in Christ's kingdom are willing to bear the insults of evil men and reach out in compassion. If you want mercy, you must give mercy.

(2) Matthew 5:21-25

In verse 21, the Lord essentially told the Jewish religious leaders, "Your rabbinical tradition says not to kill, and whosoever does kill will be in danger of judgment." That teaching was accurate but only to a point. They said that as long as you didn't murder someone, you were all right. But Jesus said, "I say unto you that whosoever is angry with his brother without a cause shall be in danger of judgment; and whosoever shall say to his brother, Raca, shall be in danger of the council; but whosoever shall say, Thou fool, shall be in danger of hell fire" (v. 22). By the way, the term *Raca* is untranslatable; it was somewhat like saying, "You brainless, stupid idiot" in a demeaning tone of voice.

To express such anger to someone is a sin. Verses 23-25 continue, "If thou bring thy gift to the altar, and there rememberest that thy brother hath anything against thee, leave there thy gift before the altar, and go thy way; first be reconciled to thy brother, and then come and offer thy gift. Agree with thine adversary quickly." You cannot come to the Lord with the concerns of your spiritual life until you've made things right with others. When you hold a grudge, you may still be able to receive instruction from God's Word, but He won't accept your worship. Who am I not to forgive someone else? If God forgave someone, I should be willing to also.

(3) Psalm 23:6

Psalm 23:6 says, "Mercy shall follow me all the days of my life." We need God's mercy all our life long because we sin. If God is so merciful, who am I to be unmerciful to others? No wonder Christianity's power is short-circuited. There are too many unresolved conflicts between people.

(4) Psalm 66:18

The psalmist wrote, "If I regard iniquity in my heart, the Lord will not hear me." Don't harbor resentment or God won't hear you.

188

(5) James 2:13

James said, "He shall have judgment without mercy, that hath shown no mercy." The Lord will chasten you if you are not merciful to others. We are to be forgiving.

A Proper Sense of Unworthiness

Commentator William Barclay tells us that when nineteenth-century Scottish author Robert Louis Stevenson lived in the South Seas, it was his habit to have his family gathered around him every day for a worship time. At the close of their time together they would say the Lord's Prayer. On one day he got halfway through the prayer, then got up and walked away. His health was always precarious, so his wife assumed that he was feeling ill and she asked him, "Is there anything wrong?" He said, "I am not fit to pray the Lord's Prayer today" (*The Gospel of Matthew*, vol. 1 [Philadelphia: Westminster, 1975], pp. 222-23). Don't come to the Lord asking for forgiveness if you know you aren't fit to do so.

(6) Matthew 18

In verses 15-17, Jesus explains that when someone in the church has sinned, you are to confront him. If attempts at reconciliation fail, you are to take one or two other people with you. If that fails, you are to tell the situation to the whole church. In response to what the Lord was teaching, Peter asked, "Lord, how often shall my brother sin against me, and I forgive him? Till seven times?" (v. 21). Peter thought he was being magnanimous to forgive seven times because the rabbis allowed three times. So Peter was doubling the rabbinical tradition plus one. Jesus said, "I say not unto thee, Until seven times; but, Until seventy times seven" (v. 22). He was saying that you are to forgive infinitely. Why? Because you are to forgive "even as God, for Christ's sake, hath forgiven you" (Eph. 4:32). And how much will He forgive you? Only 490 times? No; if that were so, you would be in real trouble if you sinned 491 times before you died. God forgives infinitely.

Christ illustrates what He is teaching in verses 23-35. Verses 23-24 begin, "Therefore is the kingdom of heaven likened unto a certain king, who would take account of his servants. And when he had begun to reckon, one was brought unto him, who owed him ten thousand talents." This particular servant owed the king ten thousand talents, which is so much money that it's hard for us to even conceive the amount. One talent was equal to six thousand denarii, and laborers earned one denarius each working day. The servant would have to work six days a week for one thousand weeks (slightly more than nineteen years) to earn *one* talent. And he owed ten thousand talents!

How could a servant ever owe that much? He may have been pilfering from the king's treasury. To become indebted to that point was almost inconceivable at that time in the history of the world. What would be roughly ten million dollars now was beyond anyone's capacity to imagine. And verse 25 says, "He had nothing with which to pay." Not only had he somehow gotten ten thousand talents, but he had also lost it all. He was a foolish person.

The only assets the servant had were his wife and children, and the king was ready to sell them into slavery to get some money back (v. 25). Then verse 26 says, "The servant, therefore, fell down, and worshiped him, saying, Lord, have patience with me, and I will pay thee all." To pay him back would have been impossible. Normally a king would be infuriated by such a response. But verse 27 tells us that "the lord of that servant was moved with compassion, and loosed him, and forgave him the debt." Now that's amazing. Whom does the king represent? God. And the servant represents us. We owe God a debt we can never pay. Yet He forgave us because He is compassionate.

In verse 28 we read this: "The same servant went out, and found one of his fellow servants, who owed him an hundred denarii." Now that was a relatively small debt; it was only the pay for three months' work. The servant who was forgiven his ten-thousand-talent debt grabbed the other man by the throat and said, "Pay me what thou owest" (v. 28). Verses 29-30 continue, "His fellow servant fell down at his feet, and besought him, saying, Have patience with me, and I will pay thee all. And he would not, but went and cast him into prison, till he should pay the debt." The debt could have been paid, but the servant who had been forgiven put the other man in jail. Now it couldn't be paid because he couldn't work for the money while in prison. That shows the evil in the first servant's heart.

The Lord continues in verses 31-35, "When his fellow servants saw what was done, they were very sorry, and came and told unto their lord all that was done. Then his lord, after he had called him, said unto him, O thou wicked servant, I forgave thee all that debt, because thou besoughtest me! Shouldest not thou also have had compassion on thy fellow servant, even as I had pity on thee? And his lord was angry, and delivered him to the inquisitors, till he should pay all that was due unto him. So likewise shall my heavenly Father do also unto you, if ye, from your hearts, forgive not every one his brother his trespasses."

That is a picture of someone who wants to receive God's forgiveness but isn't willing to forgive someone else. Do you see yourself in that illustration? Are you holding any grudges? Have you forgotten the great mercy you have received from God?

The Recipe for a Forgiving Heart

Puritan Thomas Manton said, "There is none so tender to others as they which have received mercy themselves: that know how gently God hath dealt with them." One reason you need to acknowledge your sins on a constant basis is so that you will be reminded constantly about your sinfulness and God's continual forgiveness. In the midst of that reminder, you will be more prone to forgive others. But when you fail to deal with your sins, not only will you lose your intimacy and joy with God and your usefulness to Him, but you will also become unforgiving to others because you're not being honest about what God is forgiving in your own life. Lord Herbert once said, "He who cannot forgive others breaks the bridge over which he himself must pass."

191

What have we learned? We have a problem: sin. God's provision for that is forgiveness. We receive it by confessing our sin. And the prerequisite is that we forgive others. Christianity and unforgiveness contradict one another. An unforgiving Christian is a proud, selfish person who has forgotten that his sins have been washed away. Learn to confess, and before you confess, learn to forgive.

Focusing on the Facts

1. Explain how Matthew 5:43-45 shows that Christians are to be characterized by forgiveness (see pp. 179-80).
2. What kind of example did Christ set for us in the area of forgiveness (Luke 23:34; Heb. 12:4; see p. 180)?
3. The highest act of _____ a man can display is to _____ a transgression (see p. 180).
4. According to 2 Corinthians 2:10-11, what happens when you have an unforgiving heart (see p. 181)?
5. What happens when you say, "Lord, I agree with what You say about my sin"? Explain (see p. 184).
6. What happens when you articulate your sin to the Lord in a specific manner? Why do some people avoid doing that (see p. 185)?
7. What are we to do before we seek forgiveness from God (see p. 185)?
8. What can cause a Christian to lack joy in his life (see pp. 185-86)?
9. What is the first step in dealing with a grudge (see p. 187)?
10. What will you forfeit if you don't ask for forgiveness from the person you resented (see p. 187)?
11. Why might it be helpful to give something of value to someone you have a grudge against (see p. 187)?
12. What is one reason that Christianity is short-circuited in its power (see p. 188)?
13. What will happen if you hold sin in your heart (Ps. 66:18; see p. 188)?
14. To what extent are we to be willing to forgive others (Matt. 18:21-22; see p. 189)?
15. What is the foolish servant in Matthew 18:23-35 a picture of (see pp. 189-90)?
16. What will happen when you acknowledge your sins on a constant basis? What will happen if you fail to do that (see p. 189)?

Pondering the Principles

1. It is important for Christians to be forgiving to one another, since people will fail. What would happen if Christians weren't forgiving to one another? Think of as many consequences as you can in both of these categories: (1) Person-to-person relationships and (2) the church as a whole. How would the presence of unforgiveness in a church affect an outsider's impression of that church? How would it affect his view of God? Having an unforgiving heart can have severe consequences. Memorize Ephesians 4:32, and let it remind you to always be ready to forgive others: "Be kind to one another, tender-hearted, forgiving each other, just as God in Christ also has forgiven you" (NASB).

2. Reread the section on pages 186-87 about how to remove grudges. Think of two or three people you felt bitter toward in the past. How did you handle your bitterness? Using those examples, discuss how you would have handled those situations using the guidelines presented on page 187. One aspect of removing a grudge is to give the person in question something you highly value. Determine how you would go about doing that so you can be prepared when the opportunity arises.

12
The Protection of Prayer

Outline

Introduction
A. The Contrast
B. The Centrality
C. The Criteria
D. The Claim
E. The Condition

Review
  I. God's Paternity (v. 9*a*)
 II. God's Priority (v. 9*b*)
III. God's Program (v. 10*a*)
IV. God's Plan (v. 10*b*)
 V. God's Provision (v. 11)

Lesson
 VI. God's Pardon (vv. 12, 14-15)
VII. God's Protection (v. 13*a*)
  A. The Petition
    1. The confusion
      a) Stated
      b) Simplified
    2. The collision
      a) With the natural world
      b) With the intellectual world
      c) With the emotional world
      d) With the spiritual world
    3. The clarification
      a) The allowance of temptation
      b) The avoidance of temptation
      c) The avenue of temptation
  B. The Particulars
    1. The perspective on trials
      a) They can turn into temptations

195

Introduction

In our study of Matthew 6:9-15, we've been learning how to pray. Our teacher is none other than the Lord Jesus Christ, who has given us a model for prayer. It is necessary for us to listen well and apply the things He teaches us about prayer. I know that my prayers have been reshaped to fit the pattern that the Lord has given us. The Lord's Prayer or the Disciples' Prayer is a skeleton for all prayer. The elements of this model prayer touch every area of need and every element of glorifying and praising God. It is a comprehensive masterpiece of all that is necessary in true prayer.

  A. The Contrast

      Jesus presented the Disciples' Prayer as a bold contrast to the substandard, unacceptable prayers that were common in His time. The prayers of the Pharisees were marked by hypocrisy (Matt. 6:5). They prayed standing in the synagogues and at the intersections of the streets so they would be seen by men. They were spiritual phonies who were parading themselves. The Pharisees didn't pray for the glory of God as an expression of true religion. Their prayers were hypocrisy at its worst.

      There were also pagans who prayed using vain repetition (v. 7) in hopes that their gods would hear them because of their constant speaking. The Pharisees prayed hypocritically and the pagans prayed mechanically. For the Pharisees, prayer was only a pretense of supposed piousness; for the pagans, it was a mindless routine meant to badger their gods into a response. The sin of the Pharisees was selfishness and hypocrisy, and the sin of the pagans was mindless ritualism. Jesus set over and against that the pattern for proper prayer. So our prayers are not to be said hypocritically or mechanically.

      We are never to pray for the purpose of showing off our supposed spirituality or say our prayers as a matter of routine. Yet the Lord's Prayer, which was meant to serve in contrast to hypocritical and mechanical prayer, is often used that way. Some mutter the Lord's Prayer hypocritically with hearts that are not right before God, and others say it mechanically without thinking about what they are saying. So when your heart is not right, even the Disciples' Prayer can fall into misuse.

B. The Centrality

How can you make sure your heart is right when you pray? By focusing on God when you pray. More than anything else, the Disciples' Prayer exalts God. Every phrase and petition focuses on God: His person, His attributes, and His wonderful works. To prevent our prayers from being hypocritical or mechanical, we must focus on God, not on self. That helps us avoid mindless communication.

True prayer comes from a humility that expresses absolute dependence on God. That's what our Lord wants in our prayers. The Disciples' Prayer is God-centered, not self-centered. It is truth-centered. When we think thoughts that are true about God, we will speak a prayer that seeks to glorify God. John Stott said, "When we come to God in prayer, we do not come hypocritically like play actors seeking the applause of men, nor mechanically like pagan babblers, whose mind is not in their mutterings, but thoughtfully, humbly and trustfully like little children to their Father" (*Christian Counter-Culture: The Message of the Sermon on the Mount* [Downers Grove, Ill.: InterVarsity, 1979], pp. 151-52).

C. The Criteria

Until we know the truth about God, we don't really know how to pray to Him. Hypocrites pray because they have a wrong view of God. They think they are more important than He is. Ritualists also pray from a wrong view; they don't understand that God is a God of love who desires to grant us what we need. Instead, they try to badger Him as if they had to intimidate Him into a response. In both cases, it is inadequate theology that makes their prayers substandard. When we pray, we must undergird our prayers with a concept of God that is true and comprehensive. The more you know about God, the richer and more meaningful your prayer life will become. Proper prayer will come about as you allow Scripture to form your knowledge of God. The more I know about God, the more my prayers will follow the biblical pattern.

D. The Claim

As I studied this prayer again and again in preparation for these lessons, it struck me that every petition in the prayer promises us something that God already guarantees. So when we bring those petitions to God, we aren't begging God for what is reluctantly dispensed on our behalf; rather, we are simply claiming what is already promised to us. For example, it's God's desire for His name to be hallowed, for His kingdom to come, and for His will to be done. He has already promised to give us our daily bread. He has already granted us complete forgiveness in Christ. He has promised to guide us and direct us away from evil on the path of righteousness. So when we pray, we are merely claiming what has already been promised to us. Therefore, the more we understand about the promises of God, the richer our prayers become. It's as if we have a policy with God and when we want to lay a claim, we have the right to do so. The premium has been paid by Christ, the policy is ours, the benefits are rendered on our behalf, and all we have to do is make the claim.

E. The Condition

When we meet the conditions for proper prayer, God will respond. If I pray "hallowed be thy name" but there is a lack of virtue in my life, God's name cannot be hallowed through me. But if my life is pure, I then meet the conditions for honoring His name. Likewise, when my life is pure, His kingdom will be made manifest. If I submit to God's will in obedience, His will is going to be done. If I'm living as I ought to live, He will meet my daily needs. If I have forgiven my brothers and sisters and taken care of any grudges, God will cleanse me and forgive me. If I desire to walk in the path of righteousness, He will lead me away from temptation and into the things that are right and good. As we meet the condition of prayer, we can lay claim to the promises of God. That's what true prayer is. And if we pray for something that isn't promised in God's Word, we should say, "Lord, You don't talk about this in Your Word, but I'm praying for it and am willing to accept whatever answer You give me."

Review

I. GOD'S PATERNITY (v. 9*a*; see pp. 22-31)

II. GOD'S PRIORITY (v. 9*b*; see pp. 36-49)

III. GOD'S PROGRAM (v. 10*a*; see pp. 59-69)

IV. GOD'S PLAN (v. 10*b*; see pp. 77-87, 94-107)

V. GOD'S PROVISION (v. 11; see pp. 115-24, 128-41)

VI. GOD'S PARDON (vv. 12, 14-15; see pp. 148-59, 162-75, 182-92)

Lesson

VII. GOD'S PROTECTION (v. 13*a*)

"And lead us not into temptation, but deliver us from evil."

A. The Petition

This petition speaks of God's protection. Verse 11 deals with our physical needs, verse 12 moves to our spiritual needs, and verse 13 relates to our moral needs. God takes care of our daily bread, which is our physical sustenance. He takes care of the sin in our lives by forgiving us, and He helps care for our moral standards by guiding us away from sin. Verse 12 deals with past sins, and verse 13 deals with future ones.

Are You Abusing God's Forgiveness?

If you are a true Christian, you will be just as concerned about avoiding future sins as you are about having past sins forgiven. Although everyone would be happy about having his past forgiven, a genuine expression of saving faith includes a desire for deliverance from future sins. Some people say, "I'm so glad my past sins have been forgiven. It's wonderful to know that God also keeps forgiving us. I'm going to do whatever I want and live it up. I'm going to sin so that grace may abound. Besides, I'm already forgiven anyway." I question the legitimacy of such a person's claim to salvation.

According to the Disciples' Prayer, a true son of God desires not only for his past to be forgiven but also that future sins be avoided. Why? Because to be a believer is to have a changed attitude toward sin. We are to say, "Thank you God, for forgiving my past sins, and please deliver me from future sins." The sinner whose evil past has been forgiven longs to be delivered from the tyranny of sin in the future. He knows what sin did to him in the past, and he doesn't want to get involved in it again in the future. God has been gracious to forgive the past, so don't be anxious to tread on His grace later on.

We not only need forgiveness but also deliverance. That is the cry of verse 13. The true Christian doesn't abuse God's love and force Him to constantly forgive; rather, he seeks sanctification.

1. The confusion

   a) Stated

   At first glance, the petition may seem simple: "Lead us not into temptation, but deliver us from evil." Our first reaction might be to say this petition asks God to keep us out of trouble. But upon closer examination, several questions come to mind. First, the verse begins "lead us not into temptation." Do we have to ask God to do that? Will He lead us to temptation if we don't ask Him to guide us away from it? Second, do we need to ask Him to deliver us from evil? Will He put us into evil if we don't ask for His protection?

   Some people say the word *temptation* in Matthew 6:13 means "trials." But James said, "Count it all joy when ye fall into various trials, knowing this, that the testing of your faith worketh patience. But let patience have her perfect work" (James 1:2-4). Trials aren't to be avoided; they perfect us. If we say Matthew 6:13 implies that God could lead us to temptation, we run counter to James 1:13, which says, "Let no man say when he is tempted, I am tempted of God; for God cannot be tempted with evil, neither tempteth he any man." So we can't say, "Don't tempt us." God won't do that. And we can't say, "Don't lead us into a trial" when we are to greet trials with joy.

   b) Simplified

   No matter how you deal with the word *temptation*, it seems to leave us with a problem, but that will clear up as we move along in this lesson. In his commentary on Matthew, Chrysostom, the early church Father, speaks of this petition as a natural appeal of human weakness as it faces danger (*Homily* 19.10). In other words, the petition is not as rational as it is emotional. It's a cry from the heart, and it may not be the most theologically reasoned statement. It is the utterance of one who despises the potential of sin. So it shouldn't be looked at in a precise, theological sense.

Christian character is strengthened by trials. I realize that I grow in my trials and that they are perfecting me. I also realize that God doesn't tempt me or anyone else to do something wrong. To do that would defy His own nature. Apparently verse 13 is a paradox.

That paradox is not unknown to other portions of Scripture. For example, Matthew 5:11-12 says to rejoice when you are persecuted. Yet Matthew 10:23 says to flee persecution. That's a paradox. What are you supposed to do when you are persecuted? Stand there and rejoice or run? We are to run from persecution, but when it catches us we can know joy in the midst of it.

There is a sense in which we resist a trial—there's a dread in our hearts about going through certain trials—but we know that even in the midst of those trials we will be strengthened. We know we will exercise our spiritual muscles. Trials make us better and stronger. For example, our dear Lord prayed, "O my Father, if it be possible, let this cup pass from me; nevertheless, not as I will, but as thou wilt" (Matt. 26:39). There was something in His humanness that didn't want to go to the cross. Yet it was through Christ's work on the cross that He redeemed the world. In our humanness we will say, "Lord, if You can spare me the trial, do it. But if I have to endure it, then deliver me from the potential evil that is there."

2. The collision

    The essence of this petition is based on the humility that's implied from the previous petition. We know we are sinners, and we sense our debt. Thus we say to God, "Because I have gone through the pain of confession many times and I am so battered by the fallen world that continues to collide into me, I ask You to deliver me from the possibility of sin."

    I don't know about you, but I don't trust myself. I have to set watchmen over my eyes, ears, and tongue. I'm careful about where I go, what I see, and whom I talk to about what. When I get into a trying situation, I rush into the presence of God. It's like a sentry on duty who doesn't try to fight the enemy himself but runs to tell the commander. I retreat to the presence of God and say,

"Lord, I will be overwhelmed by this situation unless You come to my aid." So the petition in Matthew 6:13 is based on self-distrust. The kingdom child realizes he lives in a fallen world that collides against him with great temptations that he, in his own humanness, cannot resist.

a)   With the natural world

There are volcanoes, earthquakes, fires, floods, pestilences, and accidents. Man is also confronted by disease and death.

b)   With the intellectual world

It is difficult for man to find the truth. His judgments are partial and unfair. His tampering with relative thinking leads to a destruction that is inevitable. Man is propelled by his own self-bias. Logic is ruled by pride, intellects are ruled by lust, and material gain makes liars out of men. There is the constant colliding of human opinions.

c)   With the emotional world

There is grief and anxiety in the world. Man's inability to handle destructive attitudes shrivels up his spirit, and his soul is chafed by his conflicts with others. Envy stings him, hate embitters him, and greed eats away at him like a canker. His affections are misplaced, his love is trampled, and his confidence is betrayed. Rich people step on the poor, and the poor seek to dethrone the rich. Prisons, hospitals, and mental institutions mark the moral and emotional upheaval of man.

d)   With the spiritual world

This is the darkest part of the picture for man. He is out of harmony with God. The machinery of man's moral nature is visibly out of gear. He is running out of sync with God's divine plan. Evil tendencies dominate man from his tainted, fallen ancestry. He may want to do right, but he feels pulled down by the irresistible gravity of evil.

Every way you look at it, we live in a fallen world. And not only is the flesh fallen, but it has to combat Satan's relentless attacks as well. Man is faced with an overpowering evil. He is divided and disheveled, prone to anything evil. We live in a fallen world, and the cry of the believer is, "God, lead me out of the evil that might come in the midst of my trials."

3. The clarification

The phrase "lead us not into temptation" brings up this question: Would God deliberately lead us into temptation? James 1:13 says, "Let no man say when he is tempted, I am tempted of God; for God cannot be tempted with evil, neither tempteth he any man." God never tempts anyone. He may allow Satan to bring trials into someone's life (Job 1:7-12), but Satan does the tempting, not God. The Lord may allow a disobedient believer in the church to be turned over to Satan "for the destruction of the flesh" (1 Cor. 5:5), but it is Satan who inflicts him, not God. He may have people "delivered unto Satan, that they may learn not to blaspheme" (1 Tim. 1:20). He permitted Christ to feel the onslaught of hell while on the cross. But He doesn't do the tempting Himself; it is only allowed in His all-encompassing will.

a) The allowance of temptation

We know God will allow us to be tempted because He is in control of everything, but He is not the source of temptation. There are times when God allows us certain trials to strengthen us, or He allows Satan to have his way in our lives because we have been disobedient and unfaithful. He allowed Satan to persecute Job to prove how righteous Job was. But God is not the tempter.

God has no association with evil, but the contrary is true for man. James 1:14 says, "Every man is tempted, when he is drawn away of his own lust, and enticed." We fall into sin when we are drawn away by our own lusts as Satan entices us. We are tempted internally by our lusts and externally by the enticement of Satan. Verse 15 continues, "When lust hath conceived, it bringeth forth sin; and sin, when it is finished, bringeth forth death."

When you are tempted and sin comes your way, remember this: "Every good gift and every perfect gift is from above, and cometh down from the Father of lights, with whom is no variableness, neither shadow of turning" (James 1:17). Every gift that God ever gives is good; that will never vary. So when evil comes, it is not from God. That is an important theological truth. People struggle with how God can allow evil. But that's His choice, and we will have to wait until eternity to find out precisely why.

b) The avoidance of temptation

God does not do evil or tempt us to do evil. Everything that proceeds from Him is good and perfect. Although He may allow evil, it isn't the expression of His heart, mind, will, or character. In fact, if you want to know how God feels about temptation, read what Jesus says in Matthew 26:41 to His disciples: "Watch and pray, that ye enter not into temptation." He wanted them to avoid it.

c) The avenue of temptation

How does Satan tempt us? According to 1 John 2:16, by the "lust of the flesh, and the lust of the eyes, and the pride of life." The verse concludes by saying that those things do not come from the Father but from the world. And they exist only by God's allowance. He gave men the liberty to choose the world or Him. He didn't make us robots who have no choice but to love Him.

In conclusion, God doesn't tempt us to do evil; rather, His desire is that we watch and pray and not enter temptation. So when you sin, don't blame God. Latin theologians used to say that lust comes *ab intra*—from the inside—or *ab extra*—from the outside (from Satan, not God).

B. The Particulars

Let's look now at what the word *temptation* means in Matthew 6:13. It is the translation of the Greek word *peirasmos*, which is frequently used in Scripture. It is a neutral word; it doesn't mean bad or good. It simply refers to a test or a trial. Now the English word *temptation* means "seduction to evil." But the word *temptation* isn't always the best translation for *peirasmos*. It can be translated "test," "prove," or "trial." A better translation for Matthew 6:13 would be the word *trial*. Then the verse would read, "Lead us not into trials."

1. The perspective on trials

a) They can turn into temptations

When we speak of a trial or a test, there is a possibility that we will pass or fail; otherwise, it isn't a test. So when God allows a trial in your life, there is always the possibility that the trial can turn into a temptation. Long after Joseph's brothers sold him into slavery in Egypt, he told them, "Ye thought evil against me; but God meant it unto good" (Gen. 50:20). Every struggle and trial we experience is allowed by God to test us, to exercise our spiritual muscles, and to help us mature. But if you don't commit the situation to God and stand in His strength, Satan will turn it into a temptation. He will entice your lusts and draw you into sin.

So the word *trial* is fitting. "Lead us not into trials" is the same as saying, "Lord, don't ever lead us into a trial that will turn into a temptation we cannot resist. Rather, deliver us from any trial that would bring evil on us as a natural consequence. Don't put us into something we can't handle." By the way, anytime you see a Greek word like *peirasmos* with the *asmos* ending, it implies a process. So we would say, "Lord, don't put us into any process or situation that is going to draw us into irresistible sin."

James clearly stated that God will not entice us to sin. A holy, sinless, absolutely righteous God will not do that. He won't tempt us into sin, but He will bring things into our lives that become tests for us. When you pass up a certain magazine, book, movie theatre, or a certain program on your television, that can be a test to show your spiritual strength. If you fail, it will turn into a temptation that incites your lust and draws you into sin.

If you're fired from a job, that may be a test. How are you going to handle it? If you take it joyously and commit your situation to the Lord, you will pass the test. But Satan will tell you, "You ought to do everything you can to ruin your boss's reputation by bad-mouthing him. Go ahead and complain to God for making things rough on you." While God is allowing a trial, Satan is trying to make it a temptation.

b) They can strengthen us

Matthew 4:1 says that Jesus was "led up by the Spirit into the wilderness to be tested." For God it was a test to prove His virtue, and for Satan it was a temptation to destroy His virtue. That's the way it will be in our trials. They will allow you to grow, and at the same time, they create the potential for sin. Job said, "When he hath tested me, I shall come forth as gold" (23:10). He approached his trial the right way. James 1:2 says, "Count it all joy when ye fall into various trials, knowing this, that the testing of your faith worketh patience. But let patience have her perfect work." Peter said, "In this ye greatly rejoice, though now for a season, if need be, ye are in heaviness through manifold trials, that the trial of your faith, being much more precious than of gold that perisheth, though it be tried with fire, might be found unto praise and honor and glory at the appearing of Jesus Christ" (1 Pet. 1:6-7).

2.   The purpose of trials

God intends trials for good, and Satan tries to turn them into evil. A trial is a test to prove your strength and exercise your spiritual muscles. God tested Abraham in the offering of Isaac (Heb. 11:17). God wanted to show what a virtuous man he was; Satan would have wanted to tempt Abraham to sin. Thus we cry out, "God, don't allow us to be led into a trial that becomes an irresistible temptation."

God plans our lives because He know what we need so that we will grow. If certain trials came to a person when he was too young in the faith, he wouldn't be able to handle them; instead, he would fall into them. There are some temptations that come to me now that I would never have been able to deal with when I was a young Christian. But as the Lord has strengthened me, He has enabled me to handle them. The Lord orders our life so that we will never be tempted without the strength to resist (1 Cor. 10:13). So Satan and the flesh are factors in the trials God brings to perfect us. The Lord uses our trials to help us trust Him more and strengthen others who go through the same trial later. He uses them to drive us to His Word and to prayer.

The petition in Matthew 6:13 is a safeguard against presumption. First Corinthians 10:12 says, "Let him that thinketh he standeth take heed lest he fall." Don't get trapped into thinking you've arrived spiritually when you haven't.

3. The preservation in trials

The word *into* is the translation of the Greek word *eis*. Some scholars have compared it to the Hebrew word *beyadh*, which means "into the power of" or "into the hands of." Using that concept in Matthew 6:13 would make it read, "Do not cause us to be led into the hands of a trial." It's one thing to be in the midst of a trial, but when we get into the hands of it, that's when it becomes a temptation. Another way of saying that would be, "As long as we're in the boat, the sea can churn all it wants. But keep us in the boat. Don't let us get into the sea or we will drown." So we ask God to keep us in His hands in the midst of a trial.

In John 17:15, our Lord prays to the Father for His disciples, saying, "I pray not that thou shouldest take them out of the world, but that thou shouldest keep them from the evil." Martin Luther said in his larger catechism on this portion of the Lord's Prayer that we cannot help being exposed to the assaults, but we pray that we may not fall or perish under them. That's the essence of Matthew 6:13. It's a prayer that asks God to defend us when we are tested, so that Satan and the flesh do not turn the test into a temptation that could lead to sin.

How Can We Deal with Temptation?

Suppose you are in the middle of a trial, and you begin to feel temptation coming. Perhaps someone has died, you've lost your job, you're angry at someone, or upset with your church. The trial may have to do with a financial, emotional, psychological, social, or spiritual matter. While the Lord is trying to help you grow, Satan begins to attack and wants to make you bitter and angry. What should you do? James 4:7 gives us a simple command: "Submit yourselves, therefore, to God."

How do you submit yourself to God? By submitting to His lordship, which means doing what He says. Submitting to God is the same thing as living in submission to biblical principles. Earlier in verse 5 James says, "Do you think that the scripture saith in vain?" How has God disclosed Himself and revealed the principles of His lordship? Through His Word. So when we are in a trial, we are to tailor our responses according to the principles of God's Word. In that way, we "resist the devil, and he will flee" (James 4:7).

Submitting to God doesn't mean getting into an emotional

trauma. It simply means ordering your life to respond in accord with the biblical revelation of God's will. So when you're in the midst of a trial, say, "God, I need Your strength and I submit to the truths of Your Word. My attitudes, actions, thoughts, and deeds are all in submission to Your Word." If you pray, "I submit to You, Lord," but your life isn't right, then your prayer won't do any good. When God's Word is hidden in your heart, you can ward off sin (Ps. 119:11). His Word is the sword that defends us against attack (Eph. 6:17). As we submit to the truths of Scripture and take up the sword of God and use it in our lives, then we resist the devil and he will flee.

C. The Protection

The petition in Matthew 6:13 recognizes the danger of living in a cursed world, where we are being battered by evil all around us. It confesses the weakness of our flesh and the absolute lack of human resource. We need the protection of our loving Father.

I don't like trials. There have been many times when I have prayed, "Lord, bring into my life what I need so that I can become the person You want me to be." But then I think, "Boy, I don't know what I'm asking for!" I'm not anxious to get into trials: I usually look forward to getting out of them. As I look over past trials, I actually become happy that they are over with. I don't like it when someone I love dies, when someone gets hurt, or when a problem comes into my life.

I don't say, "Lord, these trials are wonderful; keep them coming!" Christ didn't pray like that. He said, "Father . . . let this cup pass from me" (Matt. 26:39). But then He turned around and said in essence, "If this is what is necessary, Father, then let it be." Likewise we are to say, "Father, spare me the trial, but if it's according to your wise plan and will, then protect me so I can come out as Daniel's three friends came out of the fire without the smell of smoke [Dan. 3:27]. Let me remain untouched, as Daniel did when he walked out of the lions' den [Dan. 6:22-23]." Just as Daniel needed protection in the lions' den, so do we when we are in a trial. We can't handle trials on our own; there has to be a divine resource.

D. The Promise

Will God honor the petition in Matthew 6:13? Do you think He will protect you in trials that could become irresistible temptations? I do, based on God's promise in 1 Corinthians

10:13. Verse 12 tells us to not handle things in our own strength, then verse 13 says, "There hath no temptation taken you but such as is common to man." You won't ever face a temptation that's superhuman, nor will you face one that no one else has ever endured. God will take care of us in every trial. It would be pretty bad for us if He said, "I'll try to help you in at least one out of every ten trials."

Verse 13 continues, "God is faithful, who will not permit you to be tempted above that ye are able." You can never say, "That was too much for me." God will also "make the way to escape, that ye may be able to bear it" (v. 13). What is the way out of a trial? Through it. You have to go through a trial like you do a tunnel. If you let temptation overcome you, then you'll get derailed.

So what does 1 Corinthians 10:13 tell us? God will never allow you to experience a trial that is more than you can handle. That is seen in Matthew 6:13 in the phrase "deliver us from evil." God will never let us be tempted above what we are able to endure. That's His promise, and if we meet the condition of that promise, we can claim it. What is the condition? Submit yourself to the Lord and resist the devil.

VIII. GOD'S PREEMINENCE (v. 13b)

"For thine is the kingdom, and the power, and the glory, forever. Amen."

The Disciples' Prayer ends with that simple doxology. And a doxology is a praise offered to God. It's not meant to be analyzed or dissected.

It's possible that Jesus didn't actually say the doxology. That's why it doesn't appear in some versions of the Bible. Some ancient manuscripts have the doxology, and some don't. Nevertheless, what it says is true. The kingdom, power, and glory are God's. It seems a fitting climax to the prayer. Some commentators think Jesus did state it because the Jewish people never closed prayer on a negative note. It's an echo of 1 Chronicles 29:11. So regardless of whether Jesus said it or it was added in later manuscripts, it's true: His is the kingdom, glory, and power forever and ever.

Conclusion

What have we learned from the Lord's Prayer? All that we need is available to us. First we are to give God His rightful place. Then we can bring our needs to Him, and He will meet them through His wonderful, eternal supply.

Focusing on the Facts

1. When we pray the petitions in the Disciples' Prayer, are we begging for God to fulfill those petitions? Explain (see p. 198).
2. What are some conditions we must meet so that the Lord will respond to our prayers (see p. 198)?
3. How does a true Christian feel about committing future sins? Why (see p. 200)?
4. Why can't we pray, "God, don't tempt us" or, "God, don't lead us into a trial"? Support your answer with Scripture (see p. 200).
5. What is the paradox we encounter regarding trials? How did that paradox manifest itself in Christ's life (see pp. 200-201)?
6. What should you do when you get into a trying situation? What are you recognizing about yourself when you do that (see pp. 201-2)?
7. What is some of the proof that we live in a fallen world? Besides our fallen flesh, what else makes our walk through this world difficult (see p. 202)?
8. Does God have anything to do with the temptations we face? Explain, using Scripture to support your answer (see p. 203).
9. What does James 1:14-15 say about temptation (see p. 203)?
10. What is the significance of the words "every good gift and every perfect gift is from above" (James 1:17; see p. 203)?
11. How does God feel about temptation (Matt. 26:41; see p. 204)?
12. What is probably the best translation for the Greek word *peirasmos* in Matthew 6:13 (see p. 204)?
13. In a trial or a test, what is always a possibility? What will happen if we don't commit our trials to God (see p. 205)?
14. Cite Scripture that testifies to the strengthening effects of trials (see p. 206).
15. How did Martin Luther summarize the preservation we can seek in the midst of a trial (see p. 207)?
16. How are we to deal with temptation (James 4:7; see p. 207)?
17. What promise does the Lord give us in 1 Corinthians 10:13? What is the condition we must meet to claim that promise (see p. 206)?

Pondering the Principles

1. Second Corinthians 5:17 says, "Therefore, if any man be in Christ, he is a new creation; old things are passed away; behold, all things are become new." As Christians, we have a new

nature. But unfortunately, we live in a world flooded with evil influences. List several ways that the world presents opportunities for Christians to fall into sin (e.g., encouraging others to lie, pornographic materials, books that promote self-pride). What are some practical ways a Christian can resist such influences? When you develop habits that help you to resist the world's influence, your life will become a shining testimony for God.

2. Trials can be used as an opportunity for us to mature in Christ. What are some ways that God has used the trials in your life to strengthen you? Write down your thoughts, and take some time to thank the Lord for His work in your life.

3. When you are in a trial, James 4:7 says to submit yourself to God. That is the same thing as living in submission to what God says in His Word. What are you doing right now in your life to make sure you are living in agreement with God's Word? Are there other things you could be doing? A good way to use Scripture in the midst of a trial is to find specific passages that relate to your situation and memorize them. For guidance in doing that, you might want to seek the aid of a mature Christian, your pastor, or some good Christian books. A topical Bible can also be of great help in finding verses on specific matters.

4. As long as we are in this world, we will always face trials. Thus, a stronghold for us would be to memorize God's promise to us in 1 Corinthians 10:13. Let this verse be a comforting reminder to you whenever you encounter a trial: "No temptation has overtaken you but such as is common to man; and God is faithful, who will not allow you to be tempted beyond what you are able, but with the temptation will provide the way of escape also, that you may be able to endure it" (NASB).

Scripture Index

Moody Press, a ministry of the Moody Bible Institute, is designed for education, evangelization, and edification. If we may assist you in knowing more about Christ and the Christian life, please write us without obligation: Moody Press, c/o MLM, Chicago, Illinois 60610.